WHEN
GOD LEADS
IT MIGHT BE INTO A
DARK ALLEY

EDWINA J.H. FLYNN

WHEN GOD LEADS IT MIGHT BE INTO A DARK ALLEY

XULON PRESS

Xulon Press
2301 Lucien Way #415
Maitland, FL 32751
407.339.4217
www.xulonpress.com

Paperback ISBN-13: 978-1-66284-251-1
Ebook ISBN-13: 978-1-66284-252-8

Special Thanks

First giving thanks and honor to God my Best Friend forever who is my everything. Thanks to my husband Gawin who gave me the time to work on this project and a great big Gigantic thank you to my Project Manager Erica Coulter who held my hand and guided me through this process. Thank you Erica. Thanks to her team of editors and typesetters and the entire staff at Xulon Press. I appreciate you and God bless you all.

What Leaders Are Saying About Edwina Humphrey Flynn and This Book

When God Leads It Might Be Into A Dark Alley
- By Edwina Humphrey Flynn

Though I've known her for forty years, Edwina reveals in this book a talent I didn't know she possessed. She has been internationally renowned as a singer, and she has never disappointed. In this book her strength as a descriptive writer is put to the test, and again, she does not disappoint. As a memoir on her interesting life, we see the moving of God's gracious hand and we are inspired. This book is a treasure that can be read in one sitting or as a daily devotional, either way you will be blessed.

—-John S. Nixon, Sr., Executive Secretary,
South Central Conference of SDA

I have read your book in its entirety and re-read chapters that I found particularly meaningful for me at this time in my life.

I have to confess that I avidly "consume" three or four books on average in any given week, encompassing a wide range of topics–from historical romances to mysteries, to travel, to World History and Culture, to autobiographies of creative artists whom I admire, to biographies of icons whose lives have inspired and informed my life, to religious tomes–in a nutshell anything and everything that interests, educates and/or entertains me.

To say that your book is without doubt one of THE MOST powerful, important, absorbing, compelling, insightful, stimulating, educational, inspiring, and empowering books I have EVER read is to scratch the surface of just how much of an impact your personal relationship with God has made upon me. We have known each other since our shared Juilliard experience beginning some 50-plus years ago, (can you imagine?) and though it was clear from those memorable days that your unshakable FAITH was at the core of your LIFE and your very BEING, these amazing stories have opened my eyes to appreciate even more fully the depth and breath of your Devotion to God and your determination to LIVE YOUR LIFE as the Guide, Leader, Mentor and Teacher that His Spirit has called you to be.

I am AWED by the POWER of these testimonies and oh, SO BLESSED to have been selected to be within the circle of those honoured to call you TREASURED FRIEND for all these decades!

THANK YOU seem such inadequate words to express my overwhelming gratitude and enduring respect for your exemplary life, and for a friendship that I value as I would a rare gem, and certainly among the most important of my entire life.

With profound love and immense appreciation,

—Lorna Myers, Metropolitan Opera,
Founder/Director Voices of Harlem

Get this book! I promise you will be reading and rereading it for days to come!

—-Andrew Dawes, Manager, Sandy Spring Bank

TABLE OF CONTENTS

FOREWORD

Let's face it: we all believe in something, whether it is that the sun will come out tomorrow or our vehicle will get us safely to where we want to go or we will wake up to peace and safety in our country. So, the question is then: Who or what do we believe in at our core, our inner selves, that no one sees or knows? I've read the Holy Bible and I have read other holy books. I choose to believe in the God of that book called the Holy Bible. The Creator God of all universes is revealed in it. My belief in the Only One True God has led me into some interesting events and adventures.

During the times we live in right now with its uncertainty, COVID-19 worldwide pandemic, massive unemployment, unimaginable worldwide death toll, chaos, mayhem, murder, and all kinds of unrest and fear, it is in our best interest and need to take the time to listen to the God of Creation and closely follow His leading because He *is* who He says He is. This book shows how I learned to practice following His lead, and the interesting, surprising places God led me into! I hope you will be encouraged to listen more closely to God and not to your own understanding of what seems right and have the courage to go where He will lead you as you see what God did for me in these pages!

(*All names have been changed or left out to protect the individuals and their families mentioned in these very real experiences.*)

Before I get into a few of my personal experiences, let me tell you of a story of a man many years ago who heard God speak to him. He obeyed, and his life was saved. He was a man who loved to drink and did not believe in any god. One afternoon, he went to the next town to drink. His drinking and hanging out with the other men in the tavern lasted well into the night. At some point, however, he decided that he should start out for home. Not knowing what time it was, he stepped out into a dark and moonless night, stumbling his way to the road he thought would lead to his home. Instead, it led him into the woods. Even though he was drunk and didn't know where he was, his mind was pushing him to get home when he heard a voice telling him to stop, sit down, and rest. He kept going, thinking that he was almost home, and stumbled on his way until he heard the voice so loudly it scared him sober.

The voice said, "**Stop! Do not take another step forward. Back up and sit down until morning!**"

He obeyed, sat down, and went to sleep. When he awoke at sunrise, he realized that he was on the edge of a quarry. If he had taken one more step forward the night before, he would have plunged to certain death. He rushed to tell the parish priest, who told him he had heard the voice of God protecting him from death. God had a purpose for his life. He needed to discover what that purpose was.

Now, there are many versions of this story, but this is what I remember from when I was a kid. The point is...*Listen to God when He speaks and obey immediately*! He may be saving your life.

Many times, I have heard God speaking, telling me to make a right turn, that there was a parking space right in front of the building my appointment was in. Not only was there a parking space, but the meter was full for an entire two hours. Does God speak to us? I say **yes!** We will hear Him when we listen for His voice.

PREFACE

How do I act, think, and speak when in the presence of our great, powerful awesome Almighty God?

I will admit that some of my actions are puzzling to others and don't make sense to the average person watching me, but I've spent enough time up to this point in my life reading, studying, meditating on the Word of God, and waiting in His presence to be able to actually *hear Him speak to me!* I don't mean an impulse or a thought or feeling that I should do something, then say that's God speaking... no...I mean hearing His actual audible voice.

Believe it or not, God wants to speak to and hold conversations with *all of* His children. When I immediately follow His directives, and do what He tells me to do, things turn out *amazing!* But, when I choose to ignore or reason away what He is telling me to do, because it does not make sense to me or anyone else around me, the result turns out to be a great disaster—all the time. Without fail.

I have learned the hard way to listen and do exactly what our great God asks or tells me to do. Unfortunately, I am *still* learning to do it *immediately*! But *I am* learning and practicing to move immediately when I hear His voice.

God knows everything—really, trust and believe in that fact, as you will see in what I will be sharing.

Through this process I have become "smart enough" to believe God really *does know* everything *about everything!* And guess what? He also knows how to take care of everything as well. Now I believe with all my heart that He can take care of you and me, under any circumstances we encounter.

You know, everybody has the same privilege offered to them to be able to hear God speak to them in audible tones. I learned *and* I have taken the time to **stop, wait** and **listen** to **hear** His voice. He does not disappoint me. People, even those speaking from the pulpit, seem to be embarrassed to say in public that they hear God's voice; however, most people, even Christians—devout Christians—rarely take the time to slow down long enough to listen. We are just too busy with secular, every day, even holy day, church and family activities, to take time to stop and listen for Him to speak. Yes, but you must know too that sometimes God will let you wait before Him (even if you choose to listen) for an uncomfortable length of time to see if you're serious about waiting for Him to speak, instead of getting uncomfortable, impatient, embarrassed, angry, and running off to do your own thing or some other "more important thing" rather than sitting quietly and waiting before Almighty God. Remember the story of Mary and Martha? It's found in Luke 10:38-42. Martha was busy getting food ready for their guests and Mary sat quietly at the feet of Jesus.

Tell me now, what *is* more important than waiting for God to show up and speak to you personally? **Nothing**. I truly cannot think of anything! These things, events, and appointments (even trying to help God) that we consider more important will not save us. Only God can and will. Let's practice being in the presence of God. If you want to hear His Voice, wait there. He **will** show up for you as He does for me. As a matter of fact, He is waiting for you right now. Don't make Him wait too long.

How *do you* act, think, and speak when in the presence of the great Almighty? We have got to remember that He is always with us **all the time**, watching, caring, protecting, healing, providing, loving, and waiting for conversation with us. As the blue sky is spread above us as far as we can see and beyond, so is God's love and protection over us. Pause and think about that for a minute.

Here are a few of my many experiences that showed me just how very close God is to me, personally.

Chapter 1

IT IS SO SIMPLE, SO WHY ISN'T EVERYBODY DOING IT?

"**Y**ou must be crazy and out of your last mind!" shrieked Angelina, as I made the turn to go down the side street, the shortcut to the nearest subway station. "We all left the party to walk you to the train, but you don't appreciate our efforts to keep you safe! Do you see how dark it is down there? It's black dark. You cannot see anything down there. Where are you going? You want to die? Do you? Huh? Huh? Are you **serious**?" she yelled.

She was right of course. It *was very dark down that street!* And I never would have made the decision to take that shortcut even with a thousand bodyguards accompanying me, but I was being led down that dark street by a voice I knew, and I could not shake, so I followed the promptings and started into the darkness.

Now, let us be very clear here. I am not in the habit, anymore, of trying to ignore the voice of the Holy Spirit as He is leading me in a direction that completely goes against everything that I know to be correct. **But,** let me tell you again that it was *very, very* dark down that street. Yet, the Holy Spirit was pushing me *into* that darkness.

All my life I have been praying for and listening to and trying to follow the prompting of the Holy Spirit. Sometimes it seems strange to me, too, to do what I am being led to do, and to those watching me my actions can seem downright unsafe at times, like the minutes I am sharing with you right now. I will go into the details of this story later. What we do not seem to realize is that the **Holy Spirit** *is the only perfect protection we have on this planet.* And there are many different spirits all over the place. So, whatever **He** *is* telling us to do, we can trust

1

and believe that **He** *will* be right there to guide us and keep us safe on the mission where **He** is sending us. Whatever we need for the mission, **He** *supplies* and **He** *gives free of charge.* Do I need to **repeat that**? Strength, boldness, courage, words, skills, appearance, money, whatever is needed to get the job done to God's glory, He freely gives. So why don't we just go ahead and trust Him who is **all power and protection**?

For the life of me, I do not know why it took me so long to figure this out, either! It is so simple, but I admit, I have to practice this exercise every minute of every day, but now I hear Him. It's delightfully scary because He does not give detailed descriptions of what He wants all the time. Sometimes He does. Sometimes He doesn't. It kind of keeps me on my toes. I just know that when I follow His guidance, the result turns out to be something fabulously fantastic and marvelously amazing. I just love those moments when I can look back and say "**Wow, God**! Look at what You did!"

Chapter 2

THE RAPTURE? REALLY?

It was beautiful, but one of those hot, humid, sticky summer days in New York City. I lived near the last stop on the No. 7 train to Gun Hill Road in the Bronx. I had to walk five blocks from my apartment to the elevated train. So, I couldn't wait to get up the steps to the high platform where the breezes blew freely, not blocked by the buildings down below, where I could cool down a bit. Once on the train it was just about an eighteen-minute ride to work. Usually at this stop, as well as for a few more stops down the track, train cars were empty. For a while it seemed as if I were the only person on the train. The refreshing, cool air swirled around the empty car as the train rattled and bumped along the old tracks to its next stop. Each stop along the way, we picked up more and more people on their morning rush to get to work on time.

Soon, after a few stops, the cars began filling up with people. Well, you know what *that did*...it blocked the breeze and that made the train car hot, sticky, stuffy and most uncomfortable. I had a seat because the train was empty when I entered the car, so I had my pick of choice seats and chose one near a window. But as the people came in, some found seats, others had to stand holding on to the poles and overhead straps, silent in their own thoughts as the train sped down the tracks. I turned to face a window behind me, hoping to feel at least a little air coming in. Lost in my own thoughts, I failed to see that the car had emptied again, but I *did* notice when the cooling flow of air resume once more. When I turned to see the source of all that wonderful cooling, refreshing air, all the people had vanished.

The car was completely empty. Not one person in sight. When did *that* happen? I didn't go to sleep. I've fallen asleep on the train before. The train had not stopped anywhere, yet all the people who once were there had all gone away, it seems, in an instant. Was this the rapture and I was left behind? I was trying to be good. Why was I left behind? I was pondering in disbelief, trying to figure out the reason for the silent disappearance and why I was left alone in the car, when suddenly a "**madman**" appeared directly in front of me. This must have been why everybody ran away. They saw him and I didn't. He was a frightful sight. Now what was *I* to do?

He was standing right in front of me. His wild eyes darted here and there. Weird laughter and other strange sounds were coming from his throat. His hair was wild, messy, matted, and unkempt. There were things crawling all over him from head to toe as he slapped and scratched at them. His grinning showed multiple spaces where teeth once lived in his mouth. I could tell he had not bathed in a very, very, very long time. He was leaning on a tree branch turned into a make-shift crutch. Before I knew it, he had thrust a stinky, smelly stump of a thigh, filthily wrapped in dirty rags that were bloody and wet with unimaginable fluids, inches from my nose. The stump was crawling with all sorts of wiggly things and smelled rotten, absolutely awful. I did not even want to inhale.

As a matter of fact, things were crawling and moving all over his body, from his matted hair right down to his one bare foot and that stump he pushed in front of my face. His eyes were wild. Now, he was emitting a crazed giggle as he pushed that stump closer to my face. I sat still, silently praying. I asked for wisdom from Heaven to guide me. In a flash, I heard the Holy Spirit tell me to begin to cry.

"**What**? God, You know I have **never** been a crier. I don't cry. I would rather do something else because I hate to cry!" I said in my head. Not out loud.

The Holy Spirit said, "I will guide you, don't move a muscle! Let the silent tears fall from your eyes and ask him to sit right next to you."

"**Huh**? But he has bugs and things!" I again said in my head.

I was obedient. I did not flinch or turn away from him. I did not scream at him to get away from me. I looked up into the face of that madman and soon silent tears began flowing from my eyes. They rolled down my face and dripped from my chin into my lap.

Suddenly serious, he noticed. The grinning stopped. I motioned for him to sit down next to me. He did. Obviously in shock, but still

4

mentally examining my tear-filled eyes, he asked, not in a giggly voice, but in a very nice, manly, human voice, why I was crying. I told him I was crying because he looked like he was in a lot of pain and that it just hurt me to see him in such pain. He looked deep into my eyes. Then his eyes welled up and his tears fell silently too.

Finally, he said yes. Yes, he was in great pain all the time. It was driving him out of his mind. I asked his name and asked him to tell me his story. He did. I told him my name and introduced him to my friend Jesus, who loved him more than anyone on Earth could ever love him. We cried together and I prayed that he would accept Jesus, and he did. I asked if he had ever gotten help from anyone. He shook his head, no. Then he told me that he'd been homeless for years, and after the accident when his leg was cut off, he wrapped it as best he could with whatever cloth he could find to stop the bleeding but could not stop the incredible pain. He had never seen a doctor. I asked if I could help him. He looked at me again in shock and disbelief that I wanted to help him. No one had **ever** *offered* to help *him*. All he got was curses, things thrown at him, people screaming and running away from him. He was amazed that I was sitting calmly talking with him and was shocked that I wanted to help.

He finally said, "Please, whatever you can do, I'll gladly accept it."

I told him I knew a young doctor at a hospital near my job who I knew would help him. I asked if he would go with me to see him now. He put his head in his hands and began to weep. Then he looked up at me and said that no one had ever cared about him, they just ran from him. Yes, he would go with me to see my friend. I was praying for him all through this encounter, but now I prayed that my young doctor friend would be at the hospital when we arrived and help us. I prayed too because there were no cell phones in those years. I could not call the doctor from where we were in the subway car.

We chatted all the way to downtown Manhattan, and during the chat he asked why I didn't run away like everyone else did when he showed up. Then I told him more about my friend Jesus, who would never run from him, so neither would I.

He smiled and said, "I like your friend, and I'm glad you didn't run away."

We arrived at the corner of the block where one of the buildings of the Roosevelt Hospital was located. When I looked up from helping my new friend cross the street, I breathed a prayer of gratitude, because outside at the entry to the hospital building we were approaching was my doctor friend, talking with a group of medical personnel. See? God had already arranged it so he would be outside this particular building, and I would not have to go through the trouble of paging and trying to find him in that large hospital complex. He looked up, saw me, and called out.

"Hi there! What are you doing around here? Aren't you supposed to be at work?" he asked with grin and a wave.

I waved back. He waited until we got closer to the group and trotted over to greet us. I greeted him, then turned to introduce him to my newfound friend. I asked Doc if he could help him.

"Most certainly!" was his answer. "My brother looks like he could use a little attention," he said with a laugh and a hand on my new friend's shoulder.

Then turning to me, he told me that he had just finished his shift and was on his way to dinner, then home to rest, but first he would make sure that my new friend would get all the help he needed. He called to one of the doctors who stood watching and sent for a wheelchair to get our friend off his one foot and inside to get help. With a quick kiss on my cheek and a grin, he then whisked my homeless friend away to get the medical attention he so needed.

Some days later, he called with a report on my friend. A team of young doctors had come to help. They had taken him to an isolation room and removed those rags he used to cover himself and cut his hair and shaved him. They bathed him in a solution to remove the vermin and other creepy crawlies that were everywhere on his body. They gave him a manicure and pedicure. They debrided the stump and removed all the rotting skin, then treated and rebandaged it to start the healing. After he was cleaned up from head to toe, they gave him a soft pair of pajamas and put him in a private room to feed him, give him IV fluids, and let him rest. The next day they contacted the dental students to come and work on his mouth, and they gave him new teeth so he could eat properly.

After a few more days, my doctor friend called me and said, "You've got to come and see him. You won't recognize him at all."

After work that day, I stopped by the hospital and met my doctor friend, who took me to the room of my new friend. Doc was right. I would not have recognized him anywhere. He looked totally different, brand new, and quite handsome. He was all cleaned up and sleeping peacefully in his clean hospital bed. I didn't wake him. I stood there and watched him sleep, marveling and thanking God for the team that had done such wonderful things for this one of His children who was so much in need of help, knowing He wants to do marvelous things for all of His children, including you and me.

The social worker found him a nice furnished apartment near the hospital so he could easily come for his outpatient treatments after his discharge from the hospital. The male nurses and doctors pitched in and got him some changes of clothes and saw to it that the little restaurant near the hospital would give him his meals each day. They got him a phone in the apartment so he and I could talk with each other, and talk we did! We talked every day from the hospital at first. My project had now become their project, and they were doing a fantastic job. Soon he would be discharged from the hospital and taken to his new home and new life.

One day, my doctor friend called, asking me to dinner at our little restaurant after his shift was over. He was waiting for me, and by the time I arrived he had already ordered my favorites. During the meal, I noticed that he kept glancing at the window while giving me an update on our new man. He told me how the young doctors had befriended him, and what a brilliant and funny guy he had turned out to be. Of course, I knew this from the lively conversations we had on the phone. We talked about everything, but it was strange that he didn't want me to see him yet.

Here is the sad thing: Doc said his testing had shown he had a terminal condition, with only a few more days to live, if that many.

Wait. "**What**? He never said a word to me on the phone."

It seemed his systems were shutting down one by one, and before he couldn't stand or walk, he wanted to see me one last time before he died, but he didn't want *me* to see *him*. He thought my reaction might make him want to live, and he'd already made peace with dying and leaving the planet. So, he and Doc made the arrangement for me to come to dinner this evening where he would be able to see me, but I could not see him because of the light's reflection on the glass of the window. Doc finally quietly said that our friend had left the window.

"What? You mean he was standing there all this time and you didn't tell me?" I said in disbelief.

"That's the way he wanted it. He wouldn't have come otherwise. He just wanted to see you one last time. He also wanted you to know how much he appreciated everything you did for him, especially telling him about the love of Jesus and how you demonstrated that love for him in a very real way. He's looking forward to seeing you when Jesus comes again," Doc said.

I jumped up from the table to run toward the door, but Doc stopped me.

"He's gone," he said. "He's not there anymore. He left a few minutes ago. He does not want you to come looking for him. Just let him do this his way."

"But I would have loved to see him in his new look!" I said.

"He could not bear it if you had had the chance to visit. You have to let him go in peace," Doc said.

My heart sank. I got up from the table and went outside anyway. I called out his name, but nobody answered. The street was dark and quiet, as if I had stepped out into the *Twilight Zone*. There was no car, no bus, no people in the street. Nothing moved. This was not fair. It didn't seem real. I was hurting. I had so hoped to see the man I had brought to the hospital some weeks ago and chatted away with on the phone. I wanted to see and know the new man he had become, not just on the phone but in person. It made me sad that I would not see him anymore on this Earth, but granted him the respect he needed.

Matthew 22:37 in the New Testament says we are to love the Lord our God with all our heart, with all our soul, with all our mind and *our neighbor as ourselves*. That is a command that I have tried to live. So, I didn't run after him. I gave him his space. I know I will see him again.

"You'll just have to wait and see him in heaven," said Doc, interrupting my thoughts. "He told us you prayed for him in the subway car that day. He wants to see you in heaven. He *wants* to see *you* there."

Doc paid the check and brought me a 'doggy bag.' Outside, we wept together, holding each other close as we walked back to the hospital in silence.

"I definitely want to make it to heaven. I have got to see him there," I said. "Let's make a pact that we'll all meet together in that glorious place promised to all God's children."

Some days later, I got the call that he was gone.

I thank God that I had listened to His voice telling me what to do and leading me that warm, breezy day in the subway car where I met this man who was in so much pain it was driving him crazy. I thank God for the medical team at the Roosevelt Hospital, led by my doctor friend, who helped make his last days on Earth as pleasant as they could make them. I pray that we all will meet inside those heavenly gates and be together forevermore.

God promised and He *never* breaks His promises. The old hymn says, *When we all get to heaven, what a day of rejoicing that will be!* I can hardly wait for that day to come for so many reasons. First of all, to see Jesus face to face, God our Father, the Holy Spirit and my guardian angels (there have to be more than one angel assigned to me for various and sundry reasons), then to see all my family along with all the friends I have made during this journey on Earth.

Let me tell you something else. God had all this in mind when He prompted me to attend as a visitor, then be invited to join a discussion group of young professionals at a well-known law school in the city. The group met in one of the lounges on that campus. They were all from different schools around town, but, met together in this particular lounge to hold discussions on a variety of topics. Some of the discussions were very lively, animated, and jovial. Some were seriously somber, even sad. This young doctor friend who was kind enough to take care of the man I brought to him from my subway encounter was a member of this discussion group. See? I told you.

God knows everything about everything, and **He knows anything that can or will happen in our lives** and **He** has all the solutions, but sometimes **He** will let us partner with **Him** in amazing ways to save people and answer prayers.

Our **God is awesome!** I didn't know back then that God was leading me to join this group because He had someone who was a member of this same group who would help save a lonely child of His one day. I had only been with the group for about a year when I met the young man on the train that day. So, Doc and I already knew each other pretty well in the group from our discussions and social interactions. So, I didn't give it a second thought when the man on the train needed so much help. I prayed for my doctor friend to be around. God set it up to be that way. See? God knows everything. Trust and believe, because it is true. Guess what else? I didn't get one bug or creepy-crawly on me. Not one wriggly squirmy worm! **God is awesome!**

Chapter 3

GOD LEADS WHEN BULLETS FLY

I was on the bus, going to my new piano teacher's house for a first lesson. She lived on the other side of the Bronx from where I lived. I had to take several different trains and a couple of busses and walk four large uphill city blocks from the bus stop to get to her house, not far from the baseball stadium. It was a beautiful day for an adventure outside and I was doing well following her directions.

I got off the last bus and I heard God say, "Hit the deck!" so I dropped immediately to the sidewalk and heard the first "**Pop!**" and felt a hot whizz right over my head. I crawled back to the bus that was still sitting there and knocked on the door.

The driver looked at me and pulled off — he drove away!

God, help me! The bullets began flying all around me now and I had no cover. Again, the voice of God said for me to belly crawl around the corner. As I rounded the corner, there was a bank. Yes! Oh **no**! The bank officer was locking the door and would not open it for me, so I curled into a ball as tight as I could in the corner near the door and prepared to get struck by one of those bullets that sounded like they were coming from machine gun rounds now. I prayed to my Father in Heaven to shield me if it was not yet my time to go from this Earth.

That sound of bullets flying all around seemed to last an eternity. I don't know when the shooting stopped, but it did. I did not move a muscle. Instead, I stayed curled up in the corner of the bank entrance until someone unlocked the door and asked if I was hurt. That was when I realized it was safe to move. I answered back that I was praying, and that God had sent angels to keep me safe, so I was not harmed. I asked to use a phone to call my teacher, who promptly told me to just go back home, I was probably too shaken to focus in a lesson now. She was right.

I relaxed, then began shaking violently. The bank officer gave me a chair to sit down so I could try to pull myself together. I *know* the Angel of the Lord encamps round about us and delivers us. I saw that happen to me again and again in this big metropolis where I was now living. I praised God during the entire journey back to my house.

School was out for the summer, and I wasn't going to attend summer school, so I got a job working in an office. A corner store was across the street from the office building where I worked. I used to go over after lunch and buy my favorite chocolate candy bars for dessert. I love chocolate. I don't know why, it's just one of those things in life I need the victory over.

Anyway, I got to know the owner and several people who worked in the store. I would share short conversations and a chuckle here and there with them before heading back to the office building to work.

I went in one day and saw that very thick protection glass was installed over the counter. New security doors had been put in place as well. I didn't think too much of it because this was the big city after all, and things happened. One day, I went in to purchase my usual. The owner was there that day. When he saw me coming in, he began putting items in a bag. Then he came out from behind the protection, put an arm around me, and whispered through a kiss on my cheek, "I have given you enough chocolate bars to last you a while and I am telling you, I don't want you to come back to this store for your own safety."

He looked deep into my eyes to see if I understood. Then he gave me the biggest, tightest hug and kissed me on both cheeks and walked me to the door of his store.

I was telling the workers in the office on the first floor what had just happened to me when I saw a car pull up and begin shooting into the store where I had just been standing. Those inside the store were returning the fire right in the direction of our office. Again, I heard, "Hit the deck!" This time I was inside of a building with walls that could possibly protect, but I did not trust the walls, I trusted God. I prayed to God for His protection. And He protected everyone in the office building from flying bullets that day.

I was standing out on the deck of my home one balmy summer day, admiring the view and talking with God, when I heard, "Get down!"

Oh no, not again, I thought, as I "hit the deck," literally this time. *I'm out in the country, not in the big city. Really?*

Again, I heard the "**pop**" and felt the heat of the shell whizz past where my head had been.

God protects me when bullets fly, but even if He does not in the future, I will still trust in His protective power. I will still obey His voice speaking to me audibly.

It is a very good thing to take the time to get acquainted with the God who created us, who is also our Great King and Ruler over all things. We've heard these Christian clichés being said over the years of our existence on this planet, whether we are Christians or not, but what does that really mean? How do we take the time out of our busy schedules to get to know the One whom we cannot see or hear...or can we?

I say, "Yes, we can hear Him!" It is imperative that we do take the time and get to know our King. We're going to live with Him forever. I know for a fact He is waiting to hold audience with us. We get to go right into the throne room to meet with Him directly. Yes! Even right now through prayer. He made us. We are His children. He loves us more than we can imagine. He wants us near Him so we can talk and laugh and sing together. Forever.

That is what He has written in His love letters to us. We call those collective letters the Bible or the Holy Scriptures. Bibles are everywhere. If you don't have one, let me gently nudge you to get one and begin reading. It will literally change your life. I personally like the poetry and old English writing style of the King James Version. Pick any one version that you like and begin your reading. You'll get more than you think from just casually reading through those pages, which will spur your interest on to deeper study. Enjoy!

Chapter 4

LANGUAGE IMMERSION CONVERSION!

I was driving in from Long Island to work in Queens one morning, praying and talking with God about what might be my adventure to explore that summer, when I heard an announcement on the radio that talked about a language immersion course in the mountains of upstate New York.

Thank. You. God! This will be my new summer adventure. I am going to learn a new language. It is up in the mountains, which I love, so this will be great.

So, when I got to work, I called the State University of New York at New Paltz, New York, and promptly reserved a space for myself in their language immersion course for two weeks. The woman who answered the phone said there would be a graduation every two weeks. **Whaaaat?** She described the studies and activities I could experience there, and that was *it* for me! I could not wait for my vacation to start. I went home, packed the necessary items, put them in the trunk of my car and just waited for the date of my vacation to show up on the calendar.

The date finally arrived. I got up early. Made the ninety-minute drive up the New York State Throughway, found my exit and finally arrived on campus. Everyone was to be housed in the dorm aptly named **The Tower of Babel** because some twenty-seven or more languages, including American Sign Language, were taught during the summers. The campus was beautiful with lush lawns and huge old shade trees. A patchwork of flower beds here and there added more color to the already lovely campus grounds.

I quickly found the building where I was to register and pay for my two-week stay, which included lunch each day with my professor, being part of the requirements. Once you paid your fees, they stopped speaking to you in English or whatever your native language was, and from then on, we were *forbidden to speak in our native languages on pain of dismissal — no refund.* Oh boy! Here we go! I was going to study Spanish. I could speak zero Spanish, nor could I understand a word of it. This was going to be a fun challenge for two weeks. I hoped I would be able to eat.

After paying our fees, we were given keys to our dorm rooms, maps of the grounds and surrounding areas, and directed to the auditorium for orientation. The faculty and staff made orientation so much fun. I've never seen one like it. It was like a theater production with comedy and drama, plus a bit of music and dance thrown in for good measure. So cute! So **fun**! They had a roll call of languages. Groups of us would stand up when they called out the language we were there to study. Everyone could see how many were studying each language that would be offered this two-week session. Spanish and French were the largest groups represented during my two weeks.

Classes began precisely at 8:00 in the morning. Other activities included: movies, theater, canoeing, horseback riding, swimming, hiking, parties, going out to dinner and more, all in the language with our group and professor or class assistant. There was lab time, nap time, and time to spend alone with our studies, meditation, or just soaking in or exploring the beautiful surroundings.

At graduation, I had so much fun I wanted to do it all again.

I really did not know how much of the Spanish language I could speak and understand in two weeks, so on the suggestion of my professor, I booked a ticket to a fully Spanish-speaking country to try out my newly developing skills. I picked Mexico City. I don't know why. I didn't know at the time that God was in that selection, leading me to pick this place. Unknown to me, there was a youth congress coming to Mexico City. Christian youth from all over the world would be there the same weekend I was going to be in Mexico City, and their meetings were open to the public.

I surprised myself with how much I could understand and be understood where everyone spoke Spanish only. I walked, I shopped, I rented a car and drove, I took public transportation, found a vegetarian restaurant (I have been eating plant-based meals since birth) and ordered with ease. I chatted with the waiter, found and hung out in a park with a hundred mariachi bands. ***Wow, God****! We're doing this!* I almost said out loud. *I'm really having fun here.*

One morning I came down to the lobby of my hotel to go on an excursion and saw a group of people I recognized and some I knew.

"Hey! What are you guys doing here in Mexico City?" I asked amid hugs and screams of greeting.

They wanted to know the same about me. I told them I was exploring Mexico. Then I found out they were delegates from their churches to a worldwide youth congress being held in Mexico City that year. We arranged to meet later. I went to get my bus and continue my exploration of this great city.

I always ask God to be with me and use me for His glory each day. I never know how He's going to do that, but it **always** turns out to be an adventure.

One day, my friends from the youth congress decided to go with me to the mariachi park I had told them about. I decided we would take a taxi, so I asked the hotel concierge to call one. When the taxi came, a man looking tired and worn was driving. I noticed he had a small statue of Mary the Mother of God on his dashboard. Six of us girls climbed into the backseat of the car. The concierge had already told the driver our destination. I had not told my friends I could speak a little Spanish or that I had driven the route to the park I wanted to show them.

From our hotel it was only a fifteen-minute ride by car, but this driver started off in the wrong direction. I started to tell him he was going the wrong way but decided not to do that just yet. Hey, this was his city and maybe he knew a shorter way to the park. The Park was to the west and he was continuing east. Okaaay. This was *not* a shorter way. This guy was taking us on a "joy ride" and was up to mischief. I knew it was close to Christmas and he was putting time on his meter to drive up the price for the ride. After a while I *had* to speak up. So, I talked with him in "broken Spanish" and said I believed he was going the wrong way! No, no, he insisted he was going the right way and began going faster. In the wrong direction.

Two-and-a-half hours later (I won't say how much money), in what should have been a fifteen-minute ride, we arrived at the park entrance. This was when the Holy Spirit said to me, "Let the girls out and you stay back in the car." So, I got out and told the girls to wait for me at the gate entrance of the park. I wanted to speak to the driver. I got back in the car to pay the driver, but before I paid, I needed to talk with him about that ride. Then the Holy Spirit began speaking through me in fluent, flowing Spanish. First, I called his attention to the little statue attached to his dashboard, then I appealed to his love for Mary the Mother of God and his love for her Son, Jesus. I heard myself say that I knew it was close to Christmas time and that he was probably needing money to buy food and gifts for his wife and children but cheating other children of God was not the way to do it. It would make Mary so sad to know he was doing this. I know he didn't want to make Mary or her Son Jesus sad. If he loved God and believed that God truly would take care of him and his family, he would not cheat or do other things that would make God sad.

After speaking a few more words with him, I asked if I could pray that God would forgive him and help him take care of his family in a way pleasing to God. He said yes, removed his hat, and assumed a posture of prayer. I marveled at how the Holy Spirit prayed through me for that man and his family to be forgiven, turn from his ways, and be saved when Jesus came again. When I opened my eyes, our taxi driver was weeping. He thanked me and said how sorry he was. He asked would I please forgive him. He said through his tears that I didn't have to pay. I hugged him over the seat and told him that Jesus had already forgiven him and so did I, but don't do that again. He nodded and said, "Nunca, nunca."

Then I got out of the taxi. He refused to take the money, so I still paid him by throwing the money through the window onto the front seat near him, tip included. With that, I ran to meet the girls, who were curiously waiting for me at the gate to the park, wondering what was taking me so long. The mariachi had begun to sing.

I decided after that incident with the taxi to take the subway back to the hotel, since it was cheaper. But when we came out of the park later that evening, guess who was waiting for us? You're right. Our taxi driver. He called to me. I went to the window of the passenger side and told him thanks, but we had decided to take the train back into downtown. He said he would take us back for free. He was so sorry and ashamed of what he had done to us earlier, he asked would I please accept the free ride as his apology. I did and we all jumped back into the car. I chatted with the driver in Spanish, telling the girls what we were talking about all the way back to the hotel.

At the hotel, he said to me that he wanted to be our driver whenever we needed a taxi while we were visiting in his city. He had already spoken with the hotel concierge and made those arrangements. I accepted his offer and thanked him, but still paid him for his "free ride," tip included. God had blessed me to bless him.

I believe to this day that God prompted me to pick and arranged my trip to Mexico instead of other Spanish-speaking countries I could have chosen, to help one of His children living in Mexico City, and me, to come closer to Him. Do I believe God would do all of this for one of His own? I most certainly do. Jesus left heaven to save us. I hope to see my taxi driver with his family in heaven. I want to play with his kids there and chuckle with them about my speaking in tongues, and how their dad had understood every word.

I still pray that he will stay faithful so we will meet again inside the golden gates of God's heavenly Kingdom.

I am so glad and grateful to know I serve a God who wants to be with me all the time. Who speaks to me in audible tones Who is kind, loving, gentle, patient, protective, forgiving, fun-loving and full of exciting adventures. He never gets tired of me or bored with me. He never puts me off, he never puts me down and He loves me no matter what! I believe the word is **unconditionally**. I just gotta love Him back. Don't you think?

Chapter 5

WHEN GOD LEADS, IT MIGHT BE INTO A DARK ALLEY

"**Y**ou must be crazy and out of your *last* mind!" shrieked Angelina, as I made the turn to go down the side street, the shortcut to the nearest subway station. "We all left the party to walk you to the trains, but you don't appreciate our efforts to keep you safe! Do you see how dark it *is* down there? It's black dark. You cannot see anything down there. Where are you going? You must have a death wish. You wanna **die**? Do you? Huh? Huh? Come back right now!" she yelled after me, as I continued to walk away from them and down into the darkness. "Are you **serious**?" she screamed.

You might remember that I started to tell this story at the beginning of the book. Now you'll hear the whole thing.

She was right of course. It *was very dark down that street.* I never would have made the decision to take that shortcut even with a thousand bodyguards accompanying me, but I was being led down that dark street by a voice I knew and could not shake, so I followed the promptings and started into the darkness.

Now, I am not in the habit, anymore, of trying to ignore the voice of the Holy Spirit as He is leading me in a direction that completely goes against everything I know to be correct. It was *very, very* dark and deathly quiet down that street. Nothing moved. There were no lights in the apartment windows or over the front stoops. It was dark and I could imagine all kinds of bad things happening anyone who ventured to step into that eerie tunnel of darkness alone. Yet, the Holy Spirit was *pushing me* to go there.

Several of my friends in NYC who lived uptown in one of those huge apartments, the kind with formal dining rooms (plural) and servant's quarters, had thrown a big party. It was one of their "Y'all Come!" parties where they invited their friends as well as all the residents of their building. There was plenty of food and drink and the music was so loud, I think the bricks and steel framing of the building were moving to the beat of the music and dancing too. We were having a really good time when I noticed the clock. I had to leave. I thanked my friends for the invitation and complimented them on a great party. I told them that I was not Cinderella, but I had to get back out to Long Island before the last bus stopped running. If I missed the bus, I would be walking through three towns to get to my town plus fourteen blocks or so from the town line.

It was late evening in upper Manhattan, so some of the girls from the party decided to walk the several blocks to the subway station with me so I wouldn't have to walk it alone at that time of night. There were two possibilities for my boarding the train. One was closer than the other, but the closer station was at the very end of a very long, very dark, and very quiet street. The other one was a few more blocks down the avenue that was totally lighted, with more traffic buzzing along its street and sidewalks.

We were talking and laughing about the party. They were great company. I was so happy that they decided to come with me. When we neared the street where the closer station was, I heard the Holy Spirit say to me, "Turn down this street."

"Okay!" I said. "Here we go!"

And I started into the darkness. That was when Angelina noticed and began to shriek. They all tried to persuade me to turn back, but the Holy Spirit said, "Go forward." I shouted back at them that it was so late I was going to miss my bus, so I was going to the closer station instead.

"She's not drunk. She does not drink alcohol or do drugs. All she had was her signature drink, Perrier on the rocks with a twist of lime and that never left her hand!" Said one of the girls.

(Now, you all know my secret non-alcoholic party beverage... it's delish.)

Someone said that they'd better go with this crazy person. At least they could help me fight should anything come out of the shadows to harm me. They complained that they were missing a perfectly fabulous party to watch me get raped or murdered and cut up into a thousand pieces in that dark street. I thanked them for coming with me and suggested that we sing through the darkness. Sing we did, at the top of our lungs and in harmony. We locked arms, and in perfect step we sang our way through the darkness.

We were almost to the street light near the train station when the Holy Spirit said to me, "Stop. Turn up into this alley." Now, that alley was even darker than the street we were standing on.

I said to them, "Wait, guys, I have to see what is up in here," and I started into the alley, pulling a flashlight from my bag to see what God would be showing me.

I heard a gasp from one of the girls who followed me into the alley. The light fell on the body of a man lying on the ground amidst the rubbish and who knows what else. Listen, there are rats in New York City as large as cats and small dogs, so this man lying there was not a good thing.

I called out to him, "Sir, sir can you hear me?"

He groaned and turned his face toward the light and my friend gasped again. This time, with tears, she said in a low voice, "That's my brother! Oh my God, that's my brother!"

I shined the light in her face to see if she was kidding. The look on her face showed me she was not kidding around.

Side Bar: *The others did not know it, but this friend and I had been praying together for her oldest brother to come back home. He had left and the family didn't know where in the world he was or how he was doing. They had not seen or heard from him for years. Their mother's greatest desire was to see him again before she died. That was what we had been praying for. Prayer answered. Right here. Right now. On this dark street. Up in this even darker alley. In upper Manhattan, New York City. On my way home from a party.*

I yelled to the others and told them to call an ambulance, there was a man on the ground and he was still alive. This was before cell phones, so they went to the store on the corner and the owner called the ambulance, which came within minutes.

We rode to the hospital. Once there, I called my friend's younger brother and told him to go get his mom and meet me at the hospital. Something had happened that he would not believe unless he saw it with his own eyes. I waited in the lobby for them to arrive. My friend stayed with her brother, who had been admitted and given a room. The person at the front desk told me what room to take his family and I rushed them up without explanation. It was normal for them to have many questions because their daughter and sister was one of my best friends.

"Has there been an accident she was involved in?" they questioned.

I said nothing until we got to the room. I let them go in while I waited in the hall.

He was all cleaned up and holding his baby sister's hand when I peeked into the room. Soft muffled screams and shouts of thanksgiving to God, who had brought her son back to her, came from the mother. Everyone was hugging and kissing him and crying and praising God all at the same time. It was a great reunion. It reminded me of what we think heaven will be like when we all get there and see our family and friends and loved ones and then...when we all see **Jesus** face to face! The thought floods my eyes with tears of joy even as I am writing this right now.

My friend's brother always asked for me to be with them when they came to visit him. His sister and I had told him how we found him, and he always said with a chuckle that he was so glad I listened to God and that I was not afraid of the dark.

The family had about two more weeks with their long-lost son and brother before complications of his illness set in and began shutting down his internal organs. Each day he was showered with all the love he could stand until he peacefully passed from this life.

I was so happy that I had followed the Holy Spirit's prompting and speaking to me that night, even though I looked like a blooming idiot to those watching. Prayers were answered *and* I got a ride all the way to Long Island to my front door. I didn't even need the bus.

When God leads, it might be into an eerily dangerous, deathly quiet and very, very dark alley. But, I did not go it alone. He was right there with me all the way.

Where He leads me, I will follow. I have sung this old gospel song many times. Now I realize that He may want me to participate with Him in an answer to someone's earnest prayer and give me an unbelievable adventure at the same time as a bonus. What a God!

Chapter 6

URGENTLY NEEDED!

As I am writing these thoughts, we are in the middle of a worldwide pandemic they are calling COVID-19, a virus that has appeared upon the world's stage, and right now no one claims to know where it has come from. Theories are flying back and forth in the media and the world is in various stages of lockdown or quarantine at home all over the world. There is not a country in the world that is not affected by this virus. There has never before been a worldwide lockdown and orders for citizens to quarantine at home in the world's history. Travel is severely restricted. All civilian travel had been halted during the first weeks of this pandemic. No planes flew. No trains, busses or cars moved. Large cities around the world looked like ghost towns through the lenses of drone cameras. Eerie. Now, people are dying by the hundreds of thousands everyday around the world from COVID.

Scientists are frantic in their search to find a vaccine that will work, but they are searching in the dark because they really don't know what this virus is that they are trying to fight, nor do they know from whence it came.

People are instructed to wear masks and gloves and wash their hands and anything they touch if they venture outside of their living spaces, and to take care of themselves and others during this time. Medical teams look like personnel from a science fiction movie in their protective gear as they work near the sick and dying. Even wearing all the protective gear from head to toe, some of the doctors and nurses working around the clock, tired and bone weary, are still getting the virus themselves. Some are even dying while trying to save the lives of others. This is horrible!

Morgues cannot hold the dead and refrigerator trucks are lined up on the streets outside of hospitals and funeral homes to hold the overflow of dead bodies. Mass graves are being dug to bury them. Some countries are cremating bodies in large fires out in the open. Families are not being allowed to see their loved ones and some don't know where their dead are buried. We have never seen the likes of this before.

The leaders of our nation and our world are confused and divisive. Some people are paralyzed with fear, while other people are diabolically defiant in their unmasked hate and attacks on the civil liberties of people who do not look like them. Unashamed and uninhibited hatred of the black and brown peoples of the world are unleashed, causing unprovoked killings of black and brown peoples, even by some police and military persons who are sworn to protect the public no matter the race, ethnicity, class, or religious persuasion. There is no safety in the streets for some.

Schools are closed. Churches are closed. Eateries, restaurants, and other businesses are closed. Sports at this point are closed with stadiums empty because of the quarantine. Fear is running at an all-time high because jobs are closed, and people are wondering how to keep their homes and feed their families. Eviction notices are being delivered on a daily basis and families are being removed from their homes, most with nowhere to go. Grocery store shelves are suddenly bare from panic shopping. The economy is in a downward spiral while the numbers of the dead are soaring upward at breakneck speed. Virtual communication is the only way to talk, so meetings on computer and phone are now the new normal.

Close human touch seems to be a thing of the past, even among family members, because of social distancing. We are admonished to stay six feet apart from the next person we meet, and no hugging, kissing, fist bumping, elbow bumping or handshaking in our new greeting rituals. So, **hey**, don't touch me!

We may *not* accompany our loved ones to the doctor's office or when admitted to hospitals or nursing homes, to hold their hands when they need comfort. We *may* have window visits and wave and smile to them from outside the facility walls when possible. That is, if they are near a window.

This sounds like I'm trying to write a really bad sci fi novel or set the scene for some futuristic apocalyptic science fiction movie. **No**, I'm **not**! This is our life right now and we are living it in *real time!*

Unknown powers behind the scenes are vying for position to rule the world, not just their own countries but the entire world. Each one thinks they can do a better job at running the world, not just their own country. There is about to be a cosmic showdown such as never was since the creation of our little blue planet. It looks like it might happen in our lifetime...those living at the time of this writing. People living to be one hundred years or more have never seen anything like this in their lifetimes.

We have an urgent need to hear the voice of God speaking to us because we don't know where this is going to take us, but God does know. **He knows everything about everything,** remember? And He *will lead us* to safety.

Lord, speak to us over the noise in our minds and in the world around us. Speak to us over the loud, irregular heartbeat pounding of fear, anxiety, and dread in our chests. Speak to us over the shouts of protest and the sounds of warning gunshots and exploding tear gas grenades and falling bombs. If this continues, we may soon be living in a *"new normal"* where these rules become a bit lax and we see a sort of peace return. I read in my Bible, though, that when the leaders of the world say, "Peace, peace," then comes sudden destruction. I might live to see that come to pass. It is really crazy out there in these streets today. Speak to us, Lord, help us to hear You clearly and not be afraid to follow Your directives immediately. In Jesus' name, amen.

Chapter 7

"GO TO THE MONKEY HOUSE!"

I was walking around in a dark fog of depression that I could not seem to pull myself out of. So many events in my life at that time were shooting me down so low, I did not feel that I would ever stand up straight again. Isolated from the support of friends and family, I managed to push through and complete tasks I had to perform each day. I was determined not to become stuck in the dark quagmire of depression that can lead to despair and snatch away any desire to live on. Pray? Yes, I prayed. But got no answer.

I was going down the sidewalk on the way to the subway in New York City. I was going to work, when the group of people that hung out on this street corner noticed something was wrong, even from the distance between us. New York City sidewalks, for those who don't know, can be as wide as a two-lane road for cars in some places.

Suddenly I heard a "speech choir" saying loudly enough for the whole neighborhood to hear, "Cheer up! It can't be all *that* bad. Remember, Jesus loves you!"

It was them! These people of the New York City streets who had become my friends. I love them. I had often said those same words to them as they crowded together around a fire barrel on the corner in winter. Now, *they* were trying to cheer *me* up with those words I had said to each one of them on different occasions. I smiled and waved but kept going toward the subway station. That smile on my face was the first crack of light in my darkness.

I did not tell you before that that morning I was crying out to God, asking Him to please pull me out of the pit I was falling farther and farther down into. Somewhere inside of me I felt that I needed to laugh. I remembered what the Bible says in Proverbs 17:22, "A merry heart doeth good like a medicine, but a broken spirit drieth up the bones." I had screamed out, "God! I need a **laugh**! Can you help me with that?"

As the words flew out of my mouth, I heard my sweet Savior say to me:

"Are you **kidding Me right now**? *I* <u>made</u> your tickle box and the comedians of the jungle. **Forget work. Go directly to the monkey house at the Bronx zoo!**"

"Okay, Lord, but I really need a laugh and sometimes monkeys don't make me laugh like I think I need to laugh right now," I mumbled back to God.

"**Go to the monkey house at the zoo and you will see what I will do for you!**" I heard God say back to me. God had busted a rhyme! God was rapping to me just then! Ha! My **God is awesome!**

I immediately changed my destination route and got the train that would take me to the zoo instead. I was still feeling the heavy weight of depression pushing me down toward the sidewalk as I made my way to the entrance of the zoo and took the trail that went toward the monkey house. My back was bent downward and my breathing was labored, but not because of the strenuousness of the walk.

*Jesus, **help me**!* I screamed out in my mind.

"**Just keep going. I will meet you there!**" He said back to me.

I kept going. Soon I was inside the monkey house. It was empty. There were no people inside. The monkeys were quiet, doing their monkey things in their assigned monkey spaces. Most of the monkeys had their backs to the glass wall. After a bit of a rest on one of the benches, I went up to the glass of the first space to read the information about the residents behind that glass. I went all the way around the room, reading about the monkeys in the entire house. Then I sat on one of the benches facing one of the spaces and just waited and watched. Nothing. Nothing for a long while. I just sat there and waited to see what God wanted to show me in the monkey house at the Bronx Zoo.

"Look up in the left corner of this space, the show is about the start!" said God in a whisper.

I looked up and a large tree monkey was trotting on all fours up a bare tree trunk positioned on an upward slant. He went up on a high limb, then took the stance of an opera singer ready to perform. He stood upright, opened his mouth as if to sing, and began walking along the limb leading with his left arm, as some singers do. Suddenly he slipped, looked at me with a startled look on his face, and fell! He didn't fall far because his tail caught hold of the limb and kept him from hitting the floor. He looked back in my direction and began clapping his hands and making screeching noises while hanging and swinging back and forth by his tail. His face looked so funny!

I heard a giggle escape my lips. At that, the other monkeys, previously ignoring everything, came to life and began a performance the likes of which I had never seen before in that monkey house. Soon I was laughing so hard my cheeks hurt and tears rolled down my face. The more I laughed, the more the monkeys "cut **up**!" I laughed so hard and loud that a crowd came in to see what all the laughter was about, but it was just me laughing uncontrollably. I could feel waves of laughter rolling up from my feet to the top of my head and back down again to my toes. I laughed until my whole body ached.

"Look behind you," God said. "The show's not over! There's more."

I looked behind me at the chimpanzee space and they began a performance that had me screaming in laughter. I couldn't catch my breath. I laughed and laughed, then I laughed some more. People, curious as to what all the laughter was about, came in, saw the monkey show, and began laughing also. I laughed even more at the sound of some people's squeals, cackles, howls, hoots, guffaws, and snorts of laughter. My eyeballs were hurting. It seemed that every part of me was in immense pain from the laughter workout wrenching my entire body. I had to get out of there or I felt I would surely die laughing. I left the place still laughing so hard that people walking past me wanted to know what was so funny. All I could do was point to the monkey house! They could hear the howling laughter coming from the monkey house and ran to catch the show.

The darkness had left me. The extreme heaviness was gone. I felt as light as air. I'm sure my intermittent bursts of laughter at remembering something that had happened with the monkeys, made people on the street and on the subway think I was as crazy and out of my mind as I could be. I didn't care. I was feeling so much better now than when the day started. I felt refreshed. I felt relaxed. I felt light. I felt loved. I felt free. I felt happy, strong, and full of confidence that I could take on the world at that moment!

What a great Creator God we have! He built into us a laughter mechanism, which is one of the best tools for dealing with sickness, stress, and depression. Science and medicine back that up. They have also found that laughter is more potent than any drug and has the contagious power of a virus but has a host of great health benefits for the whole mind, the entire body and spirit. Even the side effects are all good.

Laughter releases and raises endorphin and serotonin levels, protects the heart, and relaxes the body and the mind. It even helps the body fight off infections and inflammation and has anti-aging properties. Scientific research has not yet discovered all the natural benefits of laughter. We forget how inexpensive and easy it is to apply laughter when needed No wonder the Bible says in Proverbs 17:22 a merry heart doeth good like a medicine. Science has proven that to be true. God knows. He made it, and He knows *why* He made it. He is the great Heavenly Pharmacist/Physician God. He gave that gift to us. Yes. Laughter is a gift from our great and loving God who knows the importance of having daily doses of His gift to us and what it means. They do say, people who laugh often live longest. I know they are more pleasant to be around as well as more pleasant to look at. There is no permanent scowl stamped on their faces. They seem more happy, relaxed, and healthy. You know, I think that comedians hold a special place in God's heart...Their business is humor, making people laugh. Especially if it is "clean" humor. We need them. We need comedians more than we know. They are very important people to our planet and our general health and healing.

At times, God led me to partner with Him in helping someone else...

This time *I* was the one needing God's help. This time He led me to the monkey house at the zoo and we enjoyed a thigh-slapping, foot-stomping, belly-busting, tear-jerking, high howling laugh together— God and me—together! In the Monkey House. At the **zoo**! How awesome is that? Others benefited from that zoo experience as well. My great God cares and shares.

I want more than ever to have laughter and meals, share things and places to explore that He has planned for us. I cannot wait to be in conversation face to face with Him forever. Don't you want that too?

He is the **best friend and creator God** we will ever get to know. Let's make Him our forever friend and live together with Him in eternity, He really wants that with us. He said in His Word, He does not want any of us to go to the hot place. That place was not made for us. But hey! If we choose to go to the hot place, sadly He will reluctantly let us have the desires of our hearts. Hmmm. He allows us to choose badly, even though He has made a place of unimaginable beauty and peace and rest and loveliness, adventure and fun especially for us who choose Him. 1 Corinthians 2:9 says, "Eye hath not seen nor ear heard, neither hath it entered into the heart (imagination) of man the good things which God has prepared for those who love Him." (KJV) You know, we have some amazing minds and imaginations here and now on this planet. God says that He can top that many hundreds of thousand times over!

In the meantime, remember that when God leads it just might be down a dark street or up into a darker alley. Do not fear. He will be your protection all the way. Like He said to Joshua when he was commissioned to lead the Children of Israel after Moses' death, "As I was with Moses, so I will be with you." And He **is**! He is with each one of us. Protecting us day and night. I thank Him for that each and every day. He knows just what we need...even if it is a good, hearty, healing, thigh-slapping, belly-grabbing laugh. Thank You **God** for making laughter! Thank You for making the monkeys Your comedians of the jungle! Thank You for the special gifts You have given. You put into some humans, the expertise and heart healing art of making us howl, ROTFL (rolling on the floor laughing). Clean humor is a powerful art that's needed in society today.

Chapter 8

"GET UP AND GO TO THE LOWER WEST SIDE!"

I was sleeping peacefully in my home on Long Island, New York, when I heard God gently say, "Get up and go to Manhattan on the lower west side to that new exclusive meeting place and watering hole there. Tell them **I Am** coming soon."

It was 2:00 o'clock in the morning. He told me the name of the place. I knew where it was. It was spanking brand new, really beautiful. I had driven past many times during the building and later the new owners remodeling stages, as well as after the project was finished. I could see from the street through the massive wall of windows how exquisite the place looked. It seemed only an upscale crowd met there. I could tell by the way they were dressed and the limousines that waited outside.

"I can't go in there. They won't even let me in the door. I don't live in the right zip code or have the kind of bank accounts and investment properties these people just look like they have when I look at them through the windows!"

"Come on, get up and get dressed," He said.

Okay, but You are going to have to dress me because I don't know what in my closet to wear, I said only in my head.

"I will tell you what to wear, so let's go!" He said.

I got up and showered and dressed. I went out to my car and started driving into the city. Residential Long Island was quietly sleeping on this clear and starry night, but I was headed into the city that never sleeps to the part of town where God was leading me.

"Turn down this street and park here," I heard.

I was thinking, *Okay, but it is so dark down this street, plus it is a few blocks from the destination.* Then in my overactive imagination I could see myself the center of a murder mystery. Me being the victim!

"All right. Stop that. I Am with you. Get out of the car and start walking to the Lounge. Here is what I want you to do. When you get there, enter. Go directly to the bar. Sit there. Begin to cry," He said.

"What? How am I going to do that? I don't feel sad and I'm not a crier. I do not cry," I said.

"Listen, I made your tear ducts and when you sit down at the bar those ducts I made will begin to flood water down your face, so don't worry about that," I heard Him say.

By this time, I was at the huge mahogany and glass doors. I entered, went straight to the massive bar, and sat down. Sure enough, my eyes began filling with water, which spilled right on the great wide and long mahogany bar. He said I was to put my head down and weep silently. The bartender saw me but did not say a word, only quietly put several napkins near me so I could wipe my tears, and he went on serving the patrons, not missing a beat.

Immediately, a young man came over to me and asked if I was okay. Without looking up, I just shook my head, indicating no, I was not okay. He came close and asked me what was wrong. He wanted to know if he could do anything to help me.

"Here we go!" God said. "Tell him about Me in this way. Tell him that you are not from this planet but are from a city several light years away in outer space and that you were brought here on assignment, sent from your Father, the Great and All-Powerful King I Am, who actually loves the people on this planet. He knows that there is a terrible destruction coming on Earth and that He is prepared to save all inhabitants of Earth if they would believe that He has the power to do so and are willing to be saved. He has the power to read the hearts and minds of humans from where He is, so to accept His saving power, all you have to do is think 'yes I accept.' My Father gave me the assignment to tell everyone He sends me to. I am crying because He is coming soon and I have not made my quota yet. Neither my Father nor I want any of you to be destroyed. I need to tell everyone in this room what I've just told you. My wish is that you will tell others what you have heard here tonight so that they will have the opportunity to accept or reject His saving power. He is willing to save all those who want to be saved from the coming terrors. I want you to be saved too. My Father is coming to get me soon, but if I don't complete my assignment, He will not bring me back home. I don't want Him to leave me here, I want to go home!"

The young man then turned around and addressed the large room full of people who were enjoying themselves. He interrupted their conversations and made the announcement that there was a young lady here who had something to say to them. Everyone got quiet at once. (This hardly happens, even in our churches!)

The young man tapped my shoulder and said, "There. You're on!"

I stood up, faced the crowd, and the Holy Spirit began to speak through me the story of salvation in His own way. No one booed me or ignored me to go back to their own conversations and drinks. They all remained respectfully quiet until I thanked them for listening. I told them how elated I was that they had helped me, now I could go home! I told them that all who accepted and believed my story would be saved from the destruction to come and I would see them soon. I thanked them all for graciously allowing me to interrupt their evening and help me finish my assignment so I could go home. I so longed to be there with my Father I loved so much. I waved goodbye to them and started for the door.

The young man, who had been standing by me at the bar through it all, walked me to the door. He came outside with me and said that was some terrific story. I told him that it wasn't just a story, it was the truth. He said he believed it and wanted to be saved from the destruction to come. I assured him that he would be in that number if he continued to believe.

"How did you come here?" he asked me.

"I drove," I said. "The car is just up the street."

He wanted to know if he could walk me to my car. I told him I would be safe because my Father was watching over me. I thanked him for his kind offer and his help inside. We said goodbye. When I began walking to my car, I turned and I could see through the mist that he was still outside, watching as I disappeared into the thick fog.

Now, the drive into the city was dark, the sky was clear. I could see the stars. When I left the Lounge, a thick fog had settled down. It was so thick it seemed as though someone had pulled the shades when looking out from inside the bar. Outside, I could feel the cooling mists from the fog on my skin as I walked the blocks to my car. It was very thick. I said a thank you prayer to God for this adventure with Him this morning. I was reminded of the cloud that settled amidst the children of Israel when the presence of God was there with them. As I drove through the fog, I noticed in my rearview mirror that the fog was only over the building that I had just left. I was now a block away and there was no fog. It was clear. I could see the stars again. Surely the presence of God was in that place with me, speaking through me, loving those people through me.

I pray that I will see those faces again in the heaven promised to those who love my Father too.

I have a passion to get home...to a home I have never seen. I long to be with a Father who I have never seen. I want to hug Jesus who made it possible for me to have a home here, who I have never seen. I want to see the Holy Spirit and chat with my guardian angels face to face. I know that this is all spiritual jargon, but it is more real than anything you can imagine.

The great thing is that we have the power to choose what we want to believe and in whom we want to believe. At least that's the choice my Father gives me and anyone who chooses to believe He exists. If you don't know my Father, I urge you to get to know Him. It is easy. He has told us all about Himself in ancient writings preserved thousands of years, just so you and I can get acquainted with Him. We call those writings the Holy Bible. They are everywhere. Pick up one for yourself and begin reading through it. I know you will find it as fascinating as I did and do. It is like reading through one of His diaries. If there is anything that you do not understand while reading through, just ask Him, He will tell you plainly and help you to understand.

My Father is the greatest dad ever! He loves all His children. Even the ones who do not love Him back. I cannot wait to get home to where He is right now. I know I must be patient because I learned that Father has a schedule and He sticks to it, so He will be here right on time to make His appointment to save planet Earth, you and me. I am not going to pack anything to go because my Father already has everything I will need. Let's just be ready to go. I want to finish my assignments and go **home**!

Chapter 9

WHEN GOD LEADS IT MIGHT BE TO A COOL AND SECRET PLACE

Dust puffed out in soft pinkish clouds from under my bare feet. The parched earth felt hot and crusty as I walked the red dirt path. There was no wind, not even a small breeze. The Alabama sun was high and white hot. Nothing stirred. It was too hot for flies to fly. I was seven years old and we were too poor to have air conditioning, but I knew a place where I could get cooled, even though I had to go quite far to get there.

The dirt path led through several fields of crunchy, dry brown grass. At the end of one of the fields was a row of green trees. I left the path and started across the tough, dry, dusty grass toward the patch of rich, dark green. I could hear the crunch, crunch, crunch of the grass and feel the scratchy and prickly roughness of it on the bottoms of my bare feet. The sun beat down unmercifully and turned me several shades of brown darker before I arrived at the spot.

I was so close now that I could smell the pungent aroma of the giant boxwood hedges, dense with tiny, glossy, dark green leaves. They must have been there for a hundred years or more and provided a privacy wall around the place. There was no opening. No gate. No door that I could find. The place was completely enclosed by these boxwoods. Their musty fragrance filled the air and heightened my anticipation for what I knew I would find there. I entered this other world by slipping through a small space near the ground under the boxwood. I went there so often I had carved my own secret tunnel into the place.

I noticed that the ground changed from hot and dusty to cool and moist as I belly-crawled under the giant hedges. I emerged into a cool, dark, quiet, and mysterious space that welcomed me. It was filled with huge old trees, oaks, sycamores, weeping willow and sweet magnolias. There were pine and maple trees as well. In the southwest corner was the muffled hum of bees buzzing around all kinds of fruit and nut trees, which produced yummy things to eat. All of these great trees formed the thick, cool canopy of leaves overhead, and let in small beams of light so I was not in complete darkness. Behind a small outcropping of rock, I heard the bubbling of the natural spring I found last summer. It had its own pool that I could splash around in, and the water gushing out of the rock was cold and sweet and delicious to drink.

The grass in here was soft and cool and green. A generous amount of moss grew on the trees, and more green moss on the cold stone sculptures standing about the place. I loved to lie on the cool green grass and read the elaborate poetry, witty sayings, and funny stories carved into these ancient headstones, about the people buried there. Some days I ventured up into the high branches of the trees. Cooled and hidden, I could see for miles, but no one could see me. I had prayed for cool comfort as a child and God had led me to this secret place.

When God leads, you never know what treasures you will find. He'll be right there with you, protecting you from harm and danger, as He did when I was a child. I never saw one poisonous snake or anything to harm me. When God leads, He protects!

Chapter 10

WHEN GOD LEADS IT MIGHT BE TO THE CAR DEALERSHIP

I always listen to the radio during my morning routine of getting ready for work, as do lots of people on the planet. The weather today was supposed to be bright and clear, with sunny skies. When getting dressed, I heard God tell me to wear my socks and boots and take a sweater and a coat, and put a scarf and gloves in my bag, so I did as I was told. By now, I know God is right and I just do what He says, right away.

It was a pleasant walk through a quiet, quaint residential neighborhood to the bus that would take me to my destination. The walk was about fourteen blocks to the bus stop, and I had timed the walk to reach just as the bus was pulling up to the stop, so I could walk right on and take a seat for the long ride to the next stop. I reached the bus stop on time but saw no bus coming. As I stood there waiting, the bright clear skies became a little cloudy, then a lot cloudy. Then it was dark. A chilling breeze began to blow, so I took out my sweater from my bag and put it on, thanking God that I had obeyed His voice.

Still no bus! Wait. Was that a snowflake? It sure was. Now there were more. Snow flurries? That was not mentioned in the weather report. Now it was cold and dark as twilight and the snow was really coming down. I put on my coat, hat, scarf, and gloves. Why was I still standing here? My thoughts were that the bus was just late...sometimes that happens. Now the snow was up past my ankles and the storekeeper across the street came out and shouted to me that no busses were running because a huge nor'easter was blowing in, so I better go back home while I could walk. He was watching me and gathered that I didn't have a clue as to what was about to hit the area with all the fury nature could throw at us, so he came to warn me. Then he scurried away to his home.

My walk back was treacherous. The winds were blowing hard and snow was blinding by this time, and I had many blocks more to go through a frozen tundra. My feet felt like heavy blocks of ice that did not want to move anymore. The darkening sky against the white, freshly falling snow made an eerie scene, with no one out on the streets but me. It was so quiet. I was so cold. Again, I thanked God that I had listened, but I asked Him all the way back home for a car of my own so I would not have to freeze or face unpredicted weather conditions while standing unprotected at bus stops around the town.

Finally, I reached home and put on a pot of tea. I removed my wet clothes and got into a warm shower, which I did not think would ever warm me up but finally did. In my comfy PJ's I went downstairs to the kitchen to enjoy my steamy hot cup of wonderfulness. After my hot drink, I climbed into bed and let the howling of the winds and blowing snow lull me to sleep. I dreamed of beautiful automobiles with heat in them and music playing as I drove through my dreams. Even in my sleep, I was talking with God about the possibility of having my own transportation.

The storm was one of the largest and most fierce the Northeast had seen in several years. I often wondered why God didn't just tell me to stay home that day because the storm was coming. I do know that being out in that storm for a while made me more certain about having my own transportation, and I talked with God more fervently about that subject every day. Not casually, as before the storm. I told God my preferences but of course I would take what He sent me because He knows what I need as well as what I thought I wanted.

The winter snows melted. The spring showers awakened a beautiful array of colorful flowers, the world was wonderful and warm today. My bus passed a car dealership on this route, and I dreamed of driving one of those automobiles. One day I got off the bus, went into the show room of the place and marveled at those beautiful shining machines.

Yep Lord, I would like one of these. May I have one? Please? Pretty please with a cherry on top?

I don't know why I said all that, but I did. I could because God and me—we're like that together.

After looking at all the cars in the show room, I left. I caught the next bus for the long ride to my stop, got off the bus and began walking the fourteen blocks to my house. I chatted with God in my mind all the way, thanking Him for those beauties He allowed me to experience and thanking Him for getting me home safely. Once indoors I began my evening routine, then prepared for bed. Bedtime prayers were a barrage of thank you's to God for all the blessings of the day, for gently nudging me to exit the bus home and enter the dealership show room, and the joy it brought to my day to explore each car there. I drifted off to sleep with a smile on my face and a smile in my heart.

The next morning, I awakened to God telling me to get up, my car was on the lot.

"Wait. What? Really? I mean, really? Okay God. I am going to trust You and go there today, right after work."

My work seemed light and the day flew by. Before I knew it, I was on my bus home...well, not exactly because I had a stop to make at a certain show room. My heart beat faster as the bus got closer to where I would get off and enter the show room. I was so excited to see what God was up to, because I had told God all the features that I wanted on my car. I walked through the doors and saw that the room was empty of persons. After a minute or two, a young man emerged from a back office and asked if he could help me. I told him I was there to purchase a car.

With a big broad smile, he said, "Great! I can help you with that. What are you looking for?"

He came over, shook my hand, then led me to a desk out front. I gave him my list of 'have to haves,' like the specific color, things under the hood (I needed a fast car), tires, air conditioning and heating, power windows and a moon roof and on and on. He checked my list and said that he had a car with everything but the color. I told him that color was there on his lot. Since he was the only salesman in the building, and I was his only customer, he went to check the files of the other salesmen. After a good while he came back and told me he had checked every file in the office, and sorry, no one had that color. I told him that I had it on high authority that that particular and specific car was indeed on that lot, and I wasn't leaving until we found it.

He looked at me and tapped the eraser of his pencil on the table several times, then said, "There is one more file I didn't check because it is in my manager's office. I'm going to check his file. I'll be right back."

In less than five minutes, he stuck his head out of the office door and asked, "What was that color again?" I told him. He came out of the manager's office holding a card, and with a big grin on his face said, "Come with me. I think we *do* have your car on the lot."

"I knew it!" I said as we walked out to the far back lot past a hundred cars or more. On the very last row, the very last car in the far, right corner, was my car covered with a tarp.

He pulled the tarp off and I screamed, "That's it, that's it! Thank You, God!"

God had told me to get up, my car was on the lot. Suppose I had left the show room the minute the young salesman said that he'd looked everywhere and the car I was looking for was not anywhere on the premises? I would have lost out. But I trusted the voice of my God, who speaks to me audibly and gives me the desires of my heart.

I was to come back the next afternoon and they would have the car cleaned and shined up for me to drive away, the owner of a brand new car. And it was so.

The next day when I arrived, the car was sitting inside, waiting for me to pick up the keys. A beautiful midnight blue, turbo-charged, automatic four-door Subaru sedan, complete with sun/moon roof! Before the salesman handed me the keys, we checked everything. It was all there! **God is awesome**! No more would I have to stand stranded at the bus stop in all kinds of bad weather with no way to get home. God had given me my own beautiful set of wheels that would drive me right to my door and be waiting there whenever I was ready to go anywhere. My God is **awesome**! Yes. **He is**!

God has led me to help others but has also given me some surprise gifts for myself, just for being His obedient child whom He loves.

Sometimes when God leads, it might be right into a dealer's show room with someone handing you the keys to your own shiny, spanking brand new car!

Chapter 11

WHEN GOD LEADS IT MIGHT BE TO HELP A SICK BABY

Early one morning before sunrise, I got a frantic call from a young mother who had just given birth to her first child. There were complications with the birth and the baby had to be kept in the NICU for several weeks after the mother had gone home. She visited the hospital every day, and now the day was here when she would be coming home with her precious little baby girl in her arms. She was determined to be a good mom to her little one, but soon discovered that this was not going to be as easy as she had imagined.

The first feeding time, the little baby just would not latch on to her natural feeding apparatus, she only screamed and screamed from hunger. Soon the mother was crying too. She was full of breast milk that now began dripping, still her precious baby refused to drink. All the while, she was screaming for food. Mom soon remembered that among the baby shower gifts were cans of baby formula just in case she should need it. She decided to try it. Placing the screaming baby in the crib, she ran to get the formula and tried to follow the directions as best she could through her own tears, to bring nourishment to her young one. She had forgotten that after the feeding tube was removed, the baby was introduced to the bottle in the hospital.

When she brought the bottle with the warm formula to the very loud infant, the little mouth sucked it in and became quiet. She ate her food and calmly went to sleep while the new mom had *her* meltdown. Again, the next day she tried in vain to get her little one to latch on to her, but the refusal and the screams of hunger again broke her heart.

She got the bottle of formula and fed her child while wondering what she was doing wrong.

A couple of days later, I got the panic call in the early morning hours. The baby was screaming and wouldn't stop. She would not take the bottle and her stomach was bloated and hard as a rock. The mother didn't want to take her back to the hospital. Could I come over now?

Now, I am not a nurse, nor did I have any children, but have taken care of many children up till now, babysitting for various friends and family who needed a break from parenting for a little while. I listened to the older ladies and remembered their wise remedies and what they did as help for kids in trouble.

Upon arrival and examining the baby and asking questions of the weeping mother, I discovered that the baby had not had an elimination in days! What? I spun around and told her that I would be right back, I had to get to the store immediately. By this time the sun was up, so I went to several stores in her neighborhood. Not one had what I was looking for.

In the olden days, stores used to carry baby enema bulbs. This was used to insert a little warm water into the baby's bottom to loosen up what needed to come out. I finally found a little mom-&-pop "we-sell-everything" store, and sure enough they had one. I rushed back to the house where the baby was still screaming, warmed some distilled water and slowly, gently, squeezed the warm water into the baby, who had stopped screaming at feeling the warm water flow into her little bottom. I saw a movement in her little tummy and soon baby poop was flying everywhere! The walls, the ceiling, the mother, me. Everywhere!

I went to the kitchen to look for something else while Mom was cleaning the baby, and I found it. The old nurses and midwives used to use this when babies would not nurse from their mothers. Nobody knew why it worked back then, but it did, so I was going to try it now.

The baby was clean. The room was clean. Everything was quiet when I came in from the kitchen and explained to the new mom what I wanted to try now that everyone was calm. She agreed to try whatever I wanted. Here is what she had to do.

Get some of her milk, just a drop or two, and rub the piece of sliced fresh garlic that I found in the kitchen where the baby was to suck, so the milk and garlic mixed together. I went and got the baby and handed her to her mother. I first put the baby's nose near the garlic on her mom. She opened her little mouth and latched on and began drinking her mother's nourishing food for the very first time, as it was meant to be. Big tears rolled down the mother's face as she mouthed the words "thank you" to me. I whispered that I was leaving her to have this precious bonding time with her baby. I would call her later to see how things went.

Things went very well. Soon the family began to grow and now she was a great mom having fun enjoying her children.

When we listen to God speak, we never know where He is going to send us next! It just might be to bring relief to a new mother and her sick baby.

Chapter 12

WHEN GOD LEADS TO ANOTHER NEW YORK CITY SUBWAY ENCOUNTER

Another day of classes, labs and lessons finished. It was evening and I had released my practice room to another student searching for one and was on my way home when I heard God tell me to go back to my locker, empty my bag and to stop by the cafeteria, which was closed by the way, go to the vending machines, and get food. *But I'm not hungry,* I thought. *Anyway, I'm on my way home, I can eat there.*

Then I remembered that every time I didn't obey God's voice, I got in trouble or there was a big disaster that could have been averted. So, I made a detour to the vending machines.

But, God, I don't have any money for those machines.

You know what I heard Him say?

He said, "I know that! Just do what I tell you and I will repay!"

I chuckled. "Okay, God!"

Now before this, God had told me to go to my locker and put everything in my dance bag back in my locker. These were changes of clothes, toiletries, extra shoes, books and papers I needed for homework. In other words, carry an empty bag home. Well, then He told me about the detour He wanted me to take.

I was at the first vending machine and God told me to "tap it." So, I tapped it, and everything fell down. Whoa!

"Put it in your bag," He said. "Now do the same thing with all the machines in here."

"Okay, God, but this looks like I'm stealing and..."

"You're not stealing, I said I would repay, remember? Come on, girl, hurry up!"

My bag was bulging with food and drink stuffs, so God said, "Now go home!"

I left the building and went to the subway and got on the train. It was bursting with rush-hour riders in a hurry to get home too, but a nice gentleman got up and gave me his seat. Suddenly, the train jolted to a stop and all the lights went off. This was not good and could only mean one thing...**black out!**

For those of you who don't know what this is or have never experienced one, especially in the big city on a crowded subway with a bunch of "**hangry**" people, let me tell you, it is life-threatening. It means that the power is out. Maybe in spots or maybe city-wide.

Down underground, there was no way of knowing which it was or how long the power would be out, in the days before cell phones. No matter how many times this happened to someone in the subway, it always stabbed with the cold knife of anxiety. In this case, the power was out about ten minutes before the natives began getting restless. There was pushing and shoving and cussing.

In the midst of the commotion, which was escalating by the second, God said, "Feed them."

Okay, God, I mused. *So,* this *is why all the food is in my bag!*

I always carried a flashlight before cell phones had lights in them, maybe two. I pulled out a flashlight and yelled out, "Y'all must be hungry!"

Somebody said, "She's got a light." It was pitch dark in the underground.

"All right, listen up," I said. "I've got food, but you have to share with the person next to you, okay? I have fruit, not cut up, so you have to break it in half and share...then I want you to chew it thirty-two times, okay?"

Some man over in the corner said, "Who does she think she is, my mother?"

Someone else told that person, "Hush man, she's got food!"

"Here it comes!" I said in a loud voice. "Here's an orange. Here comes an apple. Here's a sandwich and aren't you blessed it's cut in half, just right for sharing?"

I handed out bags of chips, cookies, candy, more sandwiches and juice boxes, which they had to squirt in each other's mouths to share, which started laughter and people saying, "Man, don't waste it!"

Someone said, "Get the doors! We don't have enough to share with anybody else."

Pretty soon we were all singing and laughing even though the lights were still out. Isn't God good? I commanded everyone to bow their heads and I said a blessing over the food before we ate. You know what? They did bow and the majority said "**Amen!**" when the blessing was said. Not one person objected to my prayer blessing the food.

God **did bless** that food He told me to get from the vending machines, and everyone was satisfied and laughing and talking with one another as if they were all good old friends. It was still tight in there (up to 200 people had been jammed into one subway car), but the cussing and shoving had ceased. What if I had not listened to God telling me what to do? Worse yet, what if I heard but did not do as He said? Ooo! I shudder to think.

Ya know, just because God does not give us the entire script when He asks us to do something or say something, it doesn't mean He does not know what He is doing or that He does not have a specific reason for using us in a particular way at a particular time. We forget, **God is the all-knowing, all-seeing, all-powerful God!** Just pause and think about this. He does not have time to waste with foolishness of a human kind. **His reasons** and **ways are past finding out**. We cannot know the mind of God.

It is easier to just stop what we are doing and do what He says to do, **right now**. Not next week or in an hour or two or as soon as we finish what we are doing at the moment. We need to practice immediate obedience. I am not a preacher, but I really think that this is important for us to get deep down in our spirits. I repeat. When God tells us to do something, we **must** do it immediately. Our lives or the life of someone else may depend on how quickly *we* move. In this case, it could have been murder, mayhem and massacre in the underground because of darkness, hunger, fatigue, claustrophobia, low blood sugar and rage at being in a close space, hundreds of feet underground, in between stations with no exit possible because of the **blackout**.

God told me to empty my dance bag and go fill it with food and drink. I did, and His presence went with me, before me, and surrounded me, and calmed everyone in that train car, then fed and gave them drink. **God is awesome**. I do not know why we don't love Him more and trust Him more than we do. He has already told us that He is for us and not against us, that He will never leave us or forsake us, that He is our protector and provider, our shield in time of trouble, and that only He knows the end from the beginning. Why do we not trust Him? Have you heard the story of the feeding of the 5,000 in the Bible? This was my feeding of the 200 in a dark subway car. God blessed and stretched the food He gave me to feed the hungry and give drink to the thirsty and light to those in darkness (with my trusty flashlights) that night in the dark underground subway tunnel during a **blackout in NYC**.

Chapter 13

WHEN GOD IS SILENT

I have shared a few of my intimate conversations and adventures with God my Father, Creator King of all universes. I have shared some of how and when He speaks to me, but what happens in my life when God chooses to be silent? What do I do?

Here's exactly what I do. I love Him, I sing to Him, I worship Him, I thank Him, I praise Him, I **wait**. And while waiting, I obey Him because **He is God!**

Here is what I do *not* do. I do *not* pout like a toddler, shake my little fist in His face and walk away from Him, saying, "I'm **not** your friend." I do *not* get sad with big crocodile tears rolling down my face; or sullenly give everyone, including God, the silent treatment, wearing a sour attitude that is as big as all outdoors. I do *not* get angry at Him because He did not answer me right away—maybe for a very long time. One prayer request did not get answered until twenty years later.

I do *not* throw a temper tantrum and yell and scream at God and say I will *never* talk to Him again. **No! No! A thousand times no!** I believe in a God who **is creator of everything.** I believe that He loves me and is working everything out for my good. He knows me better than I know myself. He will give me the desires of my heart if I but just wait for Him.

I look at it this way: Sometimes God just wants to cuddle in silence. Comfortable, loving, trusting, and secure in each other. Feeling each other's heartbeat, without having to say a word. I trust *Him* that way too. Why? Because He is God and I love Him. He has shown me through His Word and through His actions and through His audible voice, at times, that **He indeed can be trusted** to answer. I am sure that if you hit the replay button on your life, you can see many, many times when God has showed up in your life in such a way that everyone knows **only God** could have done it for you. Then you know, too, that God can be trusted with your life.

We are all God's children. He loves each one of us with all His heart and wants all of us to live with Him forever. Forever is a very long, long time, my friends. So, do not fret if it seems as if God is silent and not hearing your conversations with Him. He's not ignoring you, trust me, He's right next to you—sometimes carrying you, holding you, waiting for you to **trust Him** and just relax in His care. He knows the end from the beginning, remember? So, let's relax and take a chill pill because **my God**, our **God knows what He is doing** to help, protect, and save us.

Just because He may seem silent, that does not mean He is not there. Let us never forget that. God's silence means something totally different from our human silence. He is God and He is working everything out for our good. That is what He said, and He cannot lie. Patience is the key here. Active patience. While we are trusting and waiting for our answer to show up, we don't just sit and twiddle our thumbs, but we are going about our day doing the other things we know God wants us to do in the meantime. Active patience is vital to our waiting for God to speak.

Let me say something else. You know how it is when we beam in on something and our total focus is on that thing? We're God's children, so we can understand that God has the same sharp focus. So, instead of getting all bent out of shape when we don't hear specifically from God right when *we* want to hear from Him, we need to understand that **His focus is beamed in on something for our good**.

Friends, something ginormously mighty is about to happen in our lives. **Trust God** and let **Him do His thing**! Please. Don't rush Him, because we can *never know* what God knows about our situations. He can see the whole thing from another dimension. Trust that He will always work it out for our best good. We trust in a thousand other things, why not trust the one who knows everything about everything? Trust. Trust. Trust God! Yes, even when He seems silent. Wait in His presence, continuing in thanksgiving and praise, expecting to hear His voice, and you **will**! I certainly did and do hear Him speak. You will too!

Am I being redundant? You betcha I am! I want us to realize what a **great God** we have in our corner. So, being redundant? Not sorry. I'm going to keep repeating it until we all see Him face to face. I'm excited about that. Aren't you?

Chapter 14

WHEN GOD LEADS IT MIGHT BE TO BECOME CAREGIVER FOR YOUR LOVED ONE

Through a series of life events, God had been preparing me for a huge mission. I did not know it at the time, however. We rarely do know, unless God tells us up front what He's preparing to do. This time, He didn't tell me anything, I just lived through the events until one day I got the call that my dad had suffered a massive stroke and was in the ICU in a hospital hundreds of miles away from home.

Of course, we dropped everything and made the trip to the hospital. We walked into the room where he was lying there, not responding. Mom was there by his side and the rest of us stood around his bed in total shock that this strong man, minister of the Gospel of Christ, pastor of the people, who had gone into countless hospital rooms to pray for and hold the hands of the sick and the dying, was now himself hanging in the delicate balance between life and death.

We his children and our spouses, there from all over the United States, were unified in our helplessness to do anything for our dad, so we started a prayer meeting right there around his bed. We prayed, first, that God would forgive all our sins and cleanse us with the blood of Jesus and cover all of us with Christ's robe of righteousness, so that all our prayers would be heard and answered in the mighty name of Jesus our Savior. We not only prayed for Dad and Mom, but for every patient in the ICU and the entire hospital. We prayed for all the medical personnel, as well as any person working in and connected with the hospital affairs. We prayed in quiet confidence that God would hear us and heal our dad and touch every sick person in the place and give the doctors and nurses wisdom, patience, knowledge, peace, and a break as they went from patient to patient, taking care of each one during their shift. We prayed for the families of all and prayed for the salvation of all. It was a quiet but mighty time spent talking with our Father in Heaven.

God answered our prayers, for in no time Dad was walking out of the hospital and going home. The nurses in the ICU told us that there was a very sick man on a respirator in the room next to Dad, and he was taken off the ventilator the next day...he was healed. Many stories of miracles were told by the doctors and nurses of that hospital the night our family prayed.

We were told that if Dad followed all the rules, he would have a 100 percent recovery, but that he must be patient and follow the rules to the letter. One of the rules happened to be not to lift anything heavier than his fist. By now, Dad's hearing was fading, and he probably did not hear what the doctor said. He began feeling stronger, so one day he decided to lift several boxes of tiles that had been delivered and left outside the garage while he was in hospital. So, without telling anyone, he proceeded to take the boxes from outside all the way down into the basement. He was not supposed to be doing this, and after placing the last box in the basement and returning upstairs to the living room, he ended up having a seizure. This was the first of many seizures he would suffer. Thus begins my story of caregiving my parents.

I'm married, and we were living in the Washington, DC, area, getting frantic phone calls from Mom that Dad was having another seizure. She was so frightened that she was calling me instead of 911. After calming her down, I called 911 for her in their area, and an ambulance arrived within minutes to care for Dad.

At one time, I was driving up to NYC to be with them several times a month. The last time a seizure hit, I told them if he had one more seizure, I was coming up to move them to Maryland where I could keep an eye on them. He had another seizure and when Mom called that day, I told her I was coming with a truck and would be there next morning.

I called the troops and two of my brothers came and helped me load the truck. They drove it back to Maryland while I found a realtor. I put the house up for sale the same day, praying that God would sell the house for me soon. I really did want to drive to New York just one more time, and that was for the closing of the house. I did that.

The next day after moving my parents, the realtor called and said that someone just came in his office and bought the house, could we come back for the closing tomorrow? (**God is awesome! Did He answer** my prayer or **what?**) Yes! We'll make that quick U-turn and come back to get that check! Thank You, Lord.

My parents moved in with us and Dad had one or two more seizures, and then they stopped. God, my husband (who is a physician, by the way), and I worked together to get Dad back up and running (literally). In no time he was trotting around our neighborhood. Now that he was feeling better, he wanted to go back to his house!

"Say what? Naw, Baby. You can't do that."

My husband and I had a small apartment in a senior community we were going to use during retirement. When Dad wanted to be independent of me again, I promptly moved him and Mom into that place. Well, Macho Man began having seizures again, and through a series of events I had to move in with them to take care of them as their health waned more and more.

Do you think God had a hand in me being single for so much of my life, then have me marry a physician? Not just any doctor, but one He hand-picked for me because I would need his training and skills in the future. My husband was a trooper and helped tremendously in the care of our parents.

Mom eventually went blind and was paralyzed from a fall, so everything had to be done for her, including turning her every forty-five minutes so she would not get bed sores, which are the worst. Dad became feeble as well. I was elected to do every job on the planet for them, and it was my pleasure. Did I get tired? Only God knows the weariness I felt as the days went by.

I happened to go into the grocery store that was in the community about five years after both Mom and Dad died. One of the managers saw me and came over and gave me a big hug and said that they had been talking about me in the morning meeting. They wondered where I was and how I was doing. She said they were remembering me going through the store with two wheelchairs and the shopping cart. They used to stand in the window and watch me put my parents in the car and the wheelchairs in back, and then load up the groceries. That was not all. What they didn't see was that when I got back to the apartment,

I had to put them in the wheelchairs and bring them in the wheelchairs up ten steps to the walk-up apartment. Then get back to the car and bring in the groceries, take my parents out of their wheelchairs, put up groceries, and heat up a meal so the medications could be given on time. The manager didn't know all that.

One morning, I heard a voice say to me that today was the day that Dad would be leaving us. And it was so. I had worship with Dad in the emergency room on New Year's Eve, which was also the eve of the Sabbath.

At the end of prayer, I said, "Good night, Dad, I'll see you in the morning."

At that, he breathed his last breath.

A few months later, I heard God say the same about Mom. I had worship with her on the day of her event as usual. After prayer, we decided to sing a few songs. As we were singing together the song, "Jesus Loves Me," I noticed that I was singing alone. She was gone. Sometimes God leads you to take care of a loved one because there are some things that only you know how to pray for when you pray over them. I know that I will see them again if I am faithful and stay close to my Heavenly Father.

Sometimes when God leads, it is to help a loved one who cannot help themselves anymore. God will be there to hold you up all the way. Especially when He knows it will be a hard thing to do. His promise is, "I will be with you always."

Chapter 15

WHEN GOD LEADS IT sMIGHT BE TO THE RESCUE!

I n a few days, I was going on vacation. I had planned a road trip. I was going to drive from New York City down the East Coast to Miami, Florida. The trip usually took me about twelve to fourteen hours, depending on how many stops I took along the way.

I love to drive. Here's the thing, though. There is something about driving long stretches of road that makes me munchy! So, for road trips I like to pack a basket of snacks, salads, sandwiches, and a cooler with drinks, bottles of cool refreshing water, yogurt, fresh fruits and veggies. Oh, there would be cookies and cheese and crackers and a candy bar or two or three.

I would also pack meals to be cooked as I traveled down the road. I didn't like to make too many stops except for fuel and the necessary "pit stop." So, on the engine I would place my first hot meal to cook as I drove down the highway. When I began to smell the onions and peppers and mushrooms on the veggie steak, I knew lunch was ready. Veggie steak, onions, peppers and mushrooms with mashed potatoes, broccoli, cornbread and a crisp green salad in the cooler. Yum! When lunch was ready, I would pull into a rest stop, get fuel for the car, then pull over, park, and get fuel for my body. Oh yes, I had the works. Plates and eating utensils, to transfer the steaming hot food from the foil to my plate. I even packed disposable tablecloths to cover the picnic tables. I was ready for my road trip. Did I mention that I love to drive?

Armed with my playlist of traveling music, a few audio books, hand sanitizer, paper towels, and water for cleaning things, I am ready to hit the road. I always, always invite God's presence to be with me on my trips. I also ask for the presence of holy angels of God to ride with me too, so my car is jam packed as I move on down the road, with me and the heavenly Hosts.

If I timed it just right, I could get through New York City and down the New Jersey Turnpike before the traffic began to crowd the roadways and slow down my progress and before the sunrise could awaken others to begin their day.

In those days I drove an old, rebuilt police car that I bought at auction for a couple of hundred dollars. It was in perfect shape and loved the open road. Now this car could fly down the road, but I never wanted to end up in jail, so I set the cruise control to the speed limit and moved on toward my destination. One morning, however, there was a stretch of highway that had no traffic, so I decided to remove the control and open her up. Did I mention that I like to drive? Well, I also like speed! When I pressed down on the gas pedal, it was as if the car was saying to me, "Come on, girl! That's what I'm talking about. Let's go-o-o-o-o!"

I was flying low down the road and then I heard the Holy Spirit say to me, "Slow **down**! There are 'bears in the air' up over the next hill." I obeyed and slowed back down to the speed limit. Sure enough, a few miles down and over the next hill there were helicopters in the air and cruisers on the ground and officers in the road, flagging down motorists who were speeding, pulling them over and issuing tickets, I'm sure.

"Whew! Thank You, God! You let me have a little speed time and then saved me from getting a hefty ticket. There is no God like You!"

I praised God for miles down the road with singing and the spoken word. I also thanked God for the genius who built rest stops along our super-highways in this country, because after drinking water and snacking, that was just what we would be needing at pertinent intervals down the road. Such was the case here. I was happily enjoying my drive, snacking and downing bottles of water, singing, listening to music and talking with God when it became quite evident that I needed to find the next exit that had a rest stop with facilities...**stat**!

Shortly before the last exit in Virginia, God said, "Pull into the rest stop and go directly into the women's restroom."

So, at the next rest stop, I pulled in and parked right in front of the building that housed the restrooms, gift shops and restaurant. I went directly to the restroom. On my way in, I could hear a baby screaming at the top of its little lungs. The screams were coming from inside the restroom. As I entered the room, to my horror, a young lady was shaking a baby so violently that I was sure the baby was going to die right there in front of me in the next few seconds.

I heard God say, "Go take the baby from her **right now.**"

Well. I walked right over to the lady and took the baby right out of her hands, to her shock and surprise as well as to the shock of all the women who were just standing around, watching the horrible scene. What I said to her was stern and a bit harsh, but I meant every word.

"If you don't know how to love this child, give it to someone who will! You are going to **kill this baby. Do you want to do that?** I heard you telling the baby to shut up. This baby does not understand English yet...**Did you know that?**"

Now I was gently rocking the baby, who was quieting down. I was also praying fervently that God would not let the baby suffer injuries and die in my arms right then, while continuing to talk to the mother who looked tired and frazzled.

"Look," I said to her. "Your baby is no longer screaming." She reached for her child "No," I said. "Have you gone to use the toilet yet?" She indicated that she had not. While still holding her now sleeping child, I said to her, "Let's go. I'm going to stand right where you can see me through the door. I am not going anywhere with your baby. Now take your time, sit and relax a minute while we talk."

I found out that she was a brand-new mother with a three-week-old baby, and she and her husband were bringing the baby to the grandparents in Georgia. (**Not** a good idea with such a brand-new infant) They lived in New Hampshire. Mercy! Didn't her doctor tell her this was not a good idea right now and they could take the baby to visit in a few months? My thoughts were all over the place while we talked. Soon she was coming out and reaching for her baby.

"I know this is your baby, but wash your hands," I said in a low voice as I walked with her to the basin. "I know that you are really tired, and you still have quite a ways to go." She washed her hands and again reached to take her baby. I said, "Dry your hands. Come on, relax, take some time for yourself right now while the baby is sleeping. I'm right here, I'm not going anywhere. Splash your face with some refreshing cold water and put some moisturizer on your face and put on some lipstick and brush your hair. See what I'm doing? I'm gently rocking my body. Did you know that babies love that gentle motion? That's how they were rocked inside of you. So, don't ever, ever, ever shake your baby again, do you hear me? Understand? Gently rock him no matter how frustrated *you* are. He didn't ask to come here, you brought him here into this world and he needs love and affection and care from his mommy and his daddy, but I'm talking to you right now. What's his name?" I asked.

"His name is Luke," she told me. She was a bit more calm now.

"Do you know your Bible?" I asked. "Luke is a doctor in the New Testament. Read about him when you get a chance. Read about him to your little Luke. Maybe this little baby will grow up to be a doctor too!"

We both giggled at that thought. Then she turned to me for approval on her makeup and hair. The way she smiled and did a pose like a model in front of the camera, I knew she felt better.

"Well, aren't you the pretty one!" I exclaimed softly, so as not to wake the still sleeping infant. "Now," I said, "We have one more thing to do," as I led the way to the changing table and placed the sleeping baby there. "Let's change his diaper, sprinkle a little powder on him, put a clean shirt on him and you'll be good to go."

As she changed her baby, I chatted with her about the joys and challenges of motherhood. I gave her a few tips I had learned along the way, said a quick prayer for her and little Luke and his dad for safe traveling mercies and for happiness in their little family. I prayed that I would see them in God's kingdom when He comes back for His children. She picked up her bag and turned to give me a hug.

"Oh," I said, "one last thing...never turn your back on your baby, they can turn and fall in an instant." I picked up little Luke, handed him to his mom, and hugged them both, who were much calmer now than when I first came into the room. She left to join her husband who was waiting for them in the restaurant.

The women who were there when I came into the restroom were still there, watching what was going on. One of the ladies came over to me and complemented me on how I had handled the situation and asked if I were married with children of my own. I told her no, I was not married and didn't have any children. I was a college student on vacation and was driving to my destination to meet up with friends.

I need to say here, too, that I was the only brown-skinned person in the place that evening and I know there were suspicions when I strode in there and snatched that baby right out of that woman's hands. To any onlooker, that looked like trouble, but what they did not know was that God had led me to that specific rest stop at that specific time to rescue a new mother and her new baby from what could have been a horrible tragedy. We have all heard the sad stories of babies who have died as the result of "shaken baby syndrome."

As I left, I turned to look in the restaurant and there were Mom and Dad blowing kisses to me and making heart signs, saying, "Thanks, I love you!" How precious.

Back in my car, the song, "If I Can Help Somebody," came to mind. I know that Heaven in my car was singing along with me. I heard God's voice and obeyed immediately. God used me to rescue His children especially His new little one, and this was cause for **loudest praise!**

Have I told you how my praise sessions work? No? Well, I have been praising a little differently than most for quite some time now. Here it is. I praise God by telling Him *who He is* back to Himself. I separate thanksgiving from praise by thanking God *for what He has done for me and through me and situations He has brought me out* of. I'm really copying King David in the Psalms and the way he praised God and thanked God in the old King James Version of the Holy Scriptures. Here is the formula.

PRAISES	**THANKS**
I praise You Lord	I thank You Lord
Because you are:	for Saving me
Wonderful	for Loving me
Marvelous	for Healing me
Perfect Love	for Providing
Perfect Peace	for Protecting
Faithful	for Guidance
Perfect Joy	for Your Joy

Healer	For Being Ever-Present
Deliverer	for Deliverance

Get the picture? I praise by telling God who He is to me right back to Him. Isolating, separating thanksgiving and praise this way does something deep down inside of me and I cannot go back to the old way of coupling thanksgiving and praise together ever again. I have seen miracles happen when I begin to praise this way. It's amazing to me, but God has told us that He is all up inside of the praises of His people, so I should expect miraculous things to happen when I praise like that. I double dog dare you to start praising like this if you don't already. It's not easy to do, because coupling praise and thanksgiving is now part of our DNA. We have done it this way all our lives. Everybody around us does it the same way. However, in this exercise, you **must separate** the two. Praise is telling God who He is to you and thanks is gratitude for what He has done.

This is not an easy challenge. If you get it right, you win the prize. The prize is: you will get closer and closer to God. You will see His hand on you in ways you never thought you would see in all your days. Are you brave enough to take this challenge and praise this way? You will not regret it and you will never be the same again. I'm not!

Someday I may tell you some of the things that have happened in a miraculous way when I began praising God like this. Sometimes I praise out loud and sometimes in my heart. Whichever way I praise, out loud or silently, a miracle shows up. Truth! This is why I want everyone to begin praising this way. Just try it. Want to see miracles in your life? Take the challenge. But check yourself, because coupling praise and thanksgiving is so natural. Come on! Let's praise our way right up into God's Heavenly Kingdom. See you there!

Chapter 16

WHEN GOD LEADS IT MIGHT BE INTO THE LGBTQIA COMMUNITY/FAMILY

"Let me see those hands! Come on, give me your hands!" said my six-foot-four male friend while we were standing on a sidewalk outside of an eatery on Broadway in New York City.

"What? Why?" I questioned, hiding my hands behind my back.

"Girl, I've been looking at your hands all during lunch and Baby Girl, it looks like you been walking on your fingernails. They look horrible! I've never seen your nails look bad...what's going on with you?" he said, holding my hands and looking me right in the eyes. "Now, sometimes when we are going through stuff, we let parts of our appearances drop. Come by the apartment tonight and we are going to fix you up and get you right!"

"Are you guys gonna cook?" I asked him.

He gave me that "look." Yeah. Many of you know "the look." Then he said to me, "You know we always cook if we're not going out and we have some business to attend to with you tonight my dah'ling, so we will *not* be going out!" He threw his head back and laughed a good hearty laugh as only he could and said, "We're gonna cook!"

When I showed up at their apartment, the guys were ready for me. Glorious food aromas were filling the air from the elevator to their door. They fed me. The food was delicious as always and the round table chatter was hilarious! They were good company and I just loved them all.

Once the dinner dishes, etc., were cleared away, one of them asked me to step into their salon. The chair and basins were situated so that I got one friend on each hand and each foot while one massaged my scalp. I got the mani-pedi of my life. They really knew their "stuff"! They all agreed that I would have to spend the night because the massage would make me sleepy, and they could *not* have me riding the train in a sleepy stupor! My hands and feet were massaged and moisturized, and my nails polished to perfection. My scalp was tingling with the magic massage from my friend who had the hands of life. After my nails were dried, they led me to the pull-out couch and handed me a brand new, still-in-the-package-with-the-tag-still-on pajamas, robe and slippers, and said, "Go to sleep."

This was not my first visit to the "gay salon" my friends set up for me in their very spacious apartment. So, I was prepared to sleep comfortably. It was the best sleep I had had in weeks. They said good night and went off to their own beds.

I awakened to the smell of breakfast. Not just toast and coffee, but the kind of real breakfast that will really jump-start your day and carry you through it. Got dressed, ate, and thanked my friends for the love and caring support they showed me, then we all went our separate ways. This group also gave the **best** hug therapy in the world. It was a "real" thing. And yes, it was wonderful.

We shared many meals and discussions, even Bible studies when they had questions about "things." They knew that I loved God and was a Bible student myself and always had my Bible with me. I had explored other religions and read their literature and had discussions with their leaders but decided to ditch all that and go back to the Bible, which was easier for me, personally. However, one person who was new to the group sessions that we often had dismissed himself, saying that he did not want to hear anything about a God who didn't like him and wanted to send him to burn in Hell forever because he was gay. Other members of the group, who had been around me longer, convinced him to stay, because "her God is not like that!" they told him. He stayed, reluctantly. So, I turned to several texts in the Bible, let him read for himself, then we would stop and discuss, if he didn't understand what he had read. I explained to him that the God *I* had encountered in Scripture was our Creator God. He made us. Then He gave us a set of rules to follow to keep us healthy and happy. When we didn't follow those rules, we became sick and unhappy, though we might front for the public that we were so happy and content and fulfilled.

God and the Bible have been compared to a car manufacturer who sends a manual along with each car, giving specific rules of how to keep the car running smoothly. Use gasoline to run the car, not grapefruit juice, water, or milk or coffee. It will ruin the car and it will not run. Anything other than gasoline is not meant for the smooth running of that car. It is so with our Maker. When we go against those rules, the Bible calls it sin, we get sickly and are generally unhappy most of the time.

Here's the thing. God loves all of us, even though we all sin or go against His will for us and do our own thing, but He **does hate the sin** because He **knows** what going against His rules will do *to* us! He does not hate us and want to burn us in Hell. **No!** Hell is the place God made to burn up *sin,* destroy *it,* and get rid of it altogether so it never infects or comes back again. Then we can be healthy and happy forever after as He planned it in the first place. Hell was **not made for people**, but anyone who wants to cling to their sin and not let it go will have to be burned up with that sin because God hates sin and **is** going to destroy it. If you love sin and sinning so much that you refuse, you will not let it go, guess what?

And so like this the discussions would go. I didn't have to preach to them to *make them know* what *I* discovered and believed. I just loved them, and when they had questions, I would answer those specific questions to the best of my ability, or I would say I didn't know and would try to find the answer for all of us. I also told them that they had spoiled me for marriage because I didn't know a single straight man who would pamper his wife the way they pampered me. Of course, they all would laugh in agreement.

Once in one of our discussions, we talked about the latest incident in the city, where one of the members of the Community had been badly beaten and killed. I didn't know the person, but I was very upset about this senseless act of vengeance meted out on another human being. So, I asked the question: Why did members of the Community feel the need to "come out of the closet" and let everyone in the world know "who" they were and "what" they did in their private spaces? As a non-member, I couldn't see why anyone would encourage and bring onto themselves such rage, fear, uncomfortable feelings, homophobic hate and abuse by telling and showing the public who they were. I, as a woman of color, *could not change*. At first glance, anyone would know beyond the shadow of a doubt that I was a black woman. They could see that from blocks away.

"Now you may not know my way of life unless I told you. But all of you guys, if you did not advertise or come out to the world, no one would know that you live a certain and particular lifestyle. You are free to live your life any way you want. Why then do you feel it necessarily freeing to make these grand announcements to the world, telling who you are, thus inviting abuse and sometimes death?"

I wanted to know why. Everyone became eerily silent. Even the most aggressive and outspoken were quiet. Through my tears, I couldn't understand why they thought it the right thing to do to provoke danger upon themselves. Maybe even death. I just didn't understand that, because as black and brown people we are looking forward to the day when we won't have to be afraid to walk down the street and can live our lives without having to always be alert that potential harm could come to us because someone does not like the way we look, or the color of our skin brings up rage inside of them. I wanted them to know that I didn't want to lose any one of them that way. They were already free in this country. Some, more free than me! Why make these grand public announcements that provoke ignorant people to do bad things to them? I didn't understand that one. I just didn't get it.

Another very interesting discussion we had was on the power in the names of God the Father, Jesus, and the Holy Spirit. We read that God told us not to take His name in vain, meaning don't call His name for nothing!

We are given the privilege to use those names in case of **extreme need or emergencies or to give praise and thanks to God.**

"If you don't need Him, don't call his name."

"Wait. What? We do this all the time in every language on the planet!" they said.

"I know," I replied. "In every language those names are used frivolously as expletives, in anger or play or surprise, as in 'Oh my God,' 'Dios Mio,' 'Mon Dieu,' 'Jesus Christ,' 'Oh my Word,' 'Oh my goodness,' and euphemisms like 'Jeez,' 'Jee Whizz,' 'Gosh,' 'Oh my gosh,' 'OMG,' and 'Oh man.' How about this one? 'Cheese and rice,' etc. Some of these are said rather freely by devout Christians because it's 'a thing' that everyone is saying. Then Christians pick it up, not really knowing what we are doing to ourselves or to God, because in some weird way we think it's cute. Uh, excuse me, **God has no nick names!** He deserves our respect. "Hmmmm."

We all got it. It's like the story of the boy who cried "**Wolf!**"

"To keep using the names of God like this diminishes the power available for *your and my* protection, healing, and help of many kinds. Pretty soon it will mean nothing to God because just like the story of the boy," one of them said.

"Something like that, for real," I replied.

I wonder who started this. I mean calling God's name in vain, thinking it is cute. We all decided and agreed that this was sin and we had to stop doing this. Sin is anything that goes contrary to God's desire for us to live healthy, happy, prosperous, and peaceful lives, keeping us from being with Him forever. His government embodies all His commandments. (Desires) We pray the Lord's Prayer in church, saying *Thy Kingdom come*...Duh! The foundation of His Kingdom or government is His commandments...**all of them**! Including the one that says we should not take the name of the Lord our God in vain.

We all sat in silence, thinking about that one.

Then one of my friends said, "Baby Girl, we got to **stop this**! I definitely don't want to cut my own power cord from the Source! I don't think that **any of us do**!"

Then we discussed giving ourselves a challenge for two days, in which we would count the number of times in two minutes, five minutes or one hour that we used the powerful name of God in the most common and frivolous ways, just to see how often we cut our own "powerlines," hurting ourselves in this way. It turned out to be very sobering what we discovered, whether we believed it or not. We were hurting ourselves by taking God's name in vain, calling Him for nothing really and using that powerful name in cursing out another person or creature.

See? I told you that some of our discussions got really deep, sobering, and something to really think about.

Once I discovered the Lord's Day was not the one preachers and priests were telling us about, but another day altogether. The *only* day **God** had made holy, blessed, and set apart from other days as a special day to Himself. I began following *that* day in earnest because I could find nowhere in the Bible that Jesus, God, or the Holy Spirit *changed the day* **God blessed** from creation as a memorial of His work, to another day. I told my friends about this in one of our roundtable discussions. They listened and respected my findings that this day started at sunset on Fridays and ended at sunset on Saturday. I told them that as much as I deeply loved each one of them, this time was my "**hot date with God**"! I was *not* going to break that date no matter what wonderful things they had planned to include me in, so, if we were together, they would actually remind me if it was getting too close to the time for me to leave them, get home and ready for my "hot date"! Somebody would point to their watch and ask me shouldn't I be getting ready for something...like my "hot date"? These guys were so wonderful! They were caring and **real**.

They were fiercely protective of me on other counts as well, and would not let anyone say or do anything that would hurt me physically or hurt my feelings. Have you ever been "read" (the riot act) by a member of the gay community? My guys could read you without saying one curse word (they respected the fact that I did not want to hear cursing. GIGO-garbage in garbage out), but you would be ripped to shreds and have your feelings severely hurt by these expert wordsmiths when they finished with you, honey! You would leave bloodied, battered, and bruised by the barrage and bounty of blaring words aimed precisely at you to do you harm. Humm. Make you wet your pillow at night with liquid frustration because you couldn't top them!

One could hurt you. Don't let them gang up on you. You would never win. They also could and would not hesitate to physically rough you up if it came to that. Usually, it only took the words to make that other person apologize and back down. Yeah. They were 'fierce' in all senses of the word. Can you tell how much I loved them? God loved them more!

Once when all of us were out to eat, one of them spoke to the waiter and told him that I was a vegetarian and did not eat dead animals—so, no meat. He told the waiter not to cook my food with meat broth either.

When my food arrived, after saying the blessing over our food, one of my friends said, "Wait a minute! What's that pink stuff in your dish?"

I really had not seen anything in my plate, but "eagle eyes" called the waiter back to the table and asked what those pink things were.

The waiter said, "It's just a little pork for flavor. It's not meat."

Poor guy! They crucified him and sent the plate back for more appropriately prepared food for me. They didn't start eating until my plate came back without the pink stuff. Then another of my friends at the table tasted my food, then told me it was safe for me to eat because he didn't detect any "meat" taste in there. We enjoyed our meal and some great conversation and fun as always, then left the restaurant and went for a stroll down Broadway.

Once when we did this, there were so many of us, we looked like the United Nations because every race on the planet was in our group. When we walked down the street and spanned the entire New York sidewalk, several people asked if we were a choir visiting the city, to which one of the group replied, "No, we are not a choir. We're friends out for our after-dinner stroll!" Such was the deep love and tight friendship God had sent me, to help me deal with some of the dark days of my life at that time.

Our symbiotic mutualism was as natural as breathing. We didn't have to think about it, love and affection just flowed from one to another like a refreshing crystal stream.

Our discussions about the love of God got really serious when the HIV/AIDS pandemic reared its ugly head. Our conversations were raw and pertinent to what was then happening in our world. This virus, as medical professionals were calling it, seemed to be targeting the LGBTQ Community in devastating ways. Many gay friends not in our particular group were leaving us very quickly. It was disconcerting and scary to say the least. They all knew I was *practicing abstinence* in quite a few areas, and surely in the sexual arena as well. My advice to them was to simply do the same. Put aside feelings for a good cause: *saving your life!* How do you do that? Simply **decide to change your focus** from sex to something else. Find other ways to release that powerful energy. I chose God—and **swimming**! They knew I was God's child first and foremost and that my body, including my "V," belonged to **Him** and not to me. So, it was **not** mine to give to anybody who wanted to explore it or take pleasure in playing with it. I reminded them that Christ died for them too. He loved them so much He came here and died so that they could have eternal life with **Him** and share **His** pleasures forevermore. I believed this and so I'd given myself to **Him**, Christ. Me and my natural "V" and they and their perfectly well-crafted V's etc., we should trust God with our feelings and all our parts. So, we talked about the fact that they also should give Him *their* parts as well, just like I was doing, and He would keep them safe and alive if they would honor His love for them in this way. Simply put. Change your focus!

There is a verse in the Bible that says, "Let this mind be in you that was in Christ Jesus." (Phil. 2:5) If you have the mind of Christ, you will not sin because Christ lived a sinless life, being always in conversation with the Father through the Holy Spirit. He has made the communication lines so tight that all you have to do is think, "God, I'm having a bad thought, please take it away!" Right then your next thought will be something else not even near what you were thinking before. Hah! God just **changed your mind,** simply because you asked Him to. This works with all things you want to change in your life.

I was on a completely raw, no cooked foods eating plan, and was craving junk food.

I said to God, "God, *You* know what I want to eat right now, and *I* know it's not good for me. Will You please take that desire away?"

In an **instant** I was thinking about a pair of brown high heels I could wear with my outfit the next day and I didn't think about the junk food again. Isn't that just so **awesome**? We really don't have to do what's wrong if we remember to ask God to change our thoughts. We all know that thoughts lead to actions, and sometimes those actions are not right. The old folks used to say, "Jesus will fix it for you. If you let Him."

The next thing is: Practice abstinence for a good cause: life.

Well, sadly, everyone didn't have the *strength* to completely give themselves to Christ in abstinence, so many in our group succumbed to the ravages of that nasty virus as well. I sang more funerals that year than I want to remember. Forty of my friends in this precious community died in one year, including a couple of centenarians. I was crushed. But I know that they will be saved in Christ's Kingdom because our prayer sessions were real.

God knows and understands the desires of our hearts turning toward Him and He rewards that. I don't pronounce anybody as lost because I cannot read God's mind! I don't give up. I keep on praying for them.

I finally married the man God sent to me. One of my friends, who I had lost track of, was in the hospital dying and nobody told me. He left the hospital when he heard I was in town to get married. He came to the church during the wedding rehearsal. I was shocked, surprised, and so happy to see him. After our greeting, he asked if I remembered what he had told me so many years before, that was, if I **ever** *did* get married (that's another story for another time) he wanted to direct my music? Of course, I remembered. He was **fabulous!**

"Tell me what time to be here tomorrow," he said. "I can't stay for the rehearsal. I'm really very sick. But I want to do this for you because... you know, I love you and I promised."

I gave him the list of the music and the time of the wedding. He was there in rare form. The music was wonderfully directed. I didn't have to worry about a glitch in the program at all. Once again, he was there for me, even though the night before he had told me that he was in the hospital, dying from the same deadly virus, but had to stop dying to conduct the music for my wedding as he had promised years before. Did he love me? I'd say yes! He also confirmed his love for God and thanked me for my honest and sincere love for God that they could see and follow...maybe not right away...but they did.

Right after the wedding, he had to return to the hospital, where he died two days later. I will see him in heaven. This I know. God has this great way of listening and answering His children's prayers, even when it looks like He's just not going to! That's why I love *my GOD and I do not give up on HIM.* **He is awesome! He is supernatural** and not like us humans, who have gone so far away from His standards we cannot find Him again anymore. Yet He still loves us, and He knows right where *we* are! We just **don't get it!** But when we do get how much **God loves us**, what a reunion in heaven on those streets of gold we will have!

As you can see, my collection of friends in New York City was widely varied. In this group of friends were brilliant intellectuals. There were administrators, medical personnel, professors, priests, preachers, lawyers, rabbis, and business owners. Among the businesses were clothing boutiques and art galleries in the Village, and restaurants. There were musicians, dancers, Broadway and TV stars, and students like me. I pray for each one of them. I pray that we will all meet, never to part again as the Holy Scriptures promise, because I loved them all deeply and they loved me right back. They were precious to me, but even more precious to Jesus our King!

Oh, hey! I want to meet *you* there too. I'm praying for you to be there. It's okay. Even though I don't know who you are, reading this right now, God knows you, loves you and knows how to save you in His Kingdom if you *want* to be there. Now. It's your choice. Just make it an educated choice. Get to know God for yourself, then make your intelligent choice as to whether you believe the Scriptures or not. Whether you believe in Him or not. Whether you want to live God's way or not.

Don't rely on what you hear from others out there or even me. Learn for yourself. That is what I'm doing. Pray and ask God for guidance to His truth. Pray the courage to receive and accept it. Do this even if you don't believe there is a God who loves you or not. Trust me, He will still show up for you.

You know what is amazing to me? God still loves us even if we choose against Him. Did you know that?

What God, anywhere, do you know who loves like that? I don't know any. I've never heard of any, either. Our one true Creator God **is** love and His love is unbelievable until you get to know Him. Once you know Him, you will understand that His love is unbreakable and unconditional over you and me. The great preacher, Charles Haddon Spurgeon, put it this way: "trust Him Whose power is inexhaustible, Whose love is unbreakable, Whose kindness is unchangeable, Whose faithfulness is unfailing, Whose wisdom is unfathomable and Whose Goodness is impregnable." *(Devotional Material taken from Morning and Evening by C.H. Spurgeon, revised and updated by Alistair Begg. Copyright 2003, Crossway, a publishing ministry of Good News Publishers, Wheaton, IL 60187 www.crossway.org used by Truth For Life with written permission Truth For Life.org titled In Whom Do You Trust? Isaiah 36:5)*

So, somebody lied, when they put it out there that God does not care about you. That He is hard and harsh toward us and just wants to throw us in the fires of Hell with some kind of fiendish glee. Listen to me. You cannot do *anything* to make God *not* love you or for Him to withdraw His love from you. Now, don't get it twisted. We still have freedom of choice to leave Him, but He will not ever leave you. Nothing can make Him love you less. I challenge you to pick up a Holy Bible and begin to read to get to know this kind of loving God for yourself. You will quickly see what I mean. Am I being redundant? Oh well. If it helps you understand better and helps you check Him out for yourself, then good! I don't mind saying it over again.

May you make the choice to do that soon. Get to know the God I love so much. I am praying that you will love Him too, as my many friends have learned to do. You have no idea how much you are loved. Go get the book, open up your mind. You will find out how wonderful He is. It will be the best discovery you will ever make in your entire life. Guaranteed.

- If you don't know where to start, the book of John in the New Testament is a good place, then Psalms (songs), then Proverbs (a book I laughed all the way through, because my sense of humor is weird). Then, go to the first book, Genesis, and find out how you got to live here on this planet in the first place. Oh, by the way, I use the KJV (King James Version) because I like the Shakespearian style of language used, but many of my friends prefer The Clear Word or the NKJV (New King James Version) and some The Message Bible, while still others prefer the Amplified Version. Just pick one and start reading. It will be an amazing experience for you. I'm praying for you right now, asking **God** to guide you as you read His love letter to you. You can get the Bible app on your devices and listen to it being read to you as well. Whichever way you choose to explore the Bible, to discover a love like you've never known before in your life, it doesn't matter. What does matter is that you pick up a Bible and begin your journey to awesome love like you've never known before in your life.

Chapter 17

WHEN GOD LEADS IT MIGHT BE TO LOVE A TODDLER YOU DON'T KNOW

I rolled out of bed and stumbled toward the bathroom when in the first beams of dawn began to break across the sky. I rubbed my eyes because I saw a figure sitting quietly in the dark, at our dining room table down the hall. I didn't speak, neither did it. I went back to bed, and when I woke again the sun was up and the person was still sitting at the table. It was the three-year-old baby from across the street.

When I was seven years old, we moved to a little community very close to the large Air Force base outside of Montgomery, Alabama. The little bungalow my parents moved into was on a cul-de-sac where the families were very close. We soon discovered that no one locked their doors ever. We quickly became acquainted with the families and all the kids who played in the street because there was no traffic.

There was an empty house across the street from our house. One day as we all were outside playing, a taxi pulled up and turned into the driveway of that empty house. A lady and a little boy came out of the car and went into the house. We never saw them again. She didn't interact with any of the families.

One day, however, the lady came out into the front yard and filled two buckets of water and set them in the sun and went back into the house. I was curious and wondered what she was going to do with those buckets of water. Later, I watched as she came out with a basin, bathed the baby, then washed her very long hair. Hmm. Curious. This was the same baby who was sitting at our dining room table in the early morning hours. The mystery was too much for me and I had to find

73

out why this baby was in our house, dressed, when his house was right across the street. I found out that he was waiting for breakfast.

Something happened and the little boy stopped coming over and waiting for breakfast. He stopped coming out of his yard to play. One day as the kids on the block were playing a vigorous game of "No-Man-Stand," I noticed black smoke coming out of his front door. He was quietly sitting on his front lawn, hugging his knees. I ran across the street and into the house. Where was his mother? Where was the smoke coming from? The kitchen! Flames were coming from a little pot on the stove. I ran to put out the fire and open windows and doors to let out the smoke. The house was empty. His mother was not home. He had pulled a chair over to the stove and put one egg in a little pot and was trying to cook it as he had probably seen his mother do.

There was nothing in the fridge. At three years old, he did not know to put water in the pot. The baby was hungry. Why didn't he come and eat at our house anymore? We had food. I picked him up and carried him to our house and gave him something to eat. He didn't speak much, but the big smile on his face was all the thanks I needed. I carried him back to his house when I went to check to see if the smoke had cleared and to close the windows and doors I had opened in the house. I looked around and saw only a table and a chair, a bed for his mother, and a little bed for him in another room. There were no clothes in the closet and no toiletries in the bathroom. I flicked the light switch to see in the closet and soon found out that there was no electricity. The gas stovetop had one little pot on it and that was now burned to a crisp. Oh, the reason she was bathing the baby and washing her hair outside was becoming clear to me now. She was warming the water in the sun.

I was seven years old, but I made this baby my project. Most of the parents were at work during the day, except one or two moms who had just had babies. Maybe his mother had to work too. But she left him all alone. All day. Why had he stopped coming to our house to eat breakfast? We always had a big breakfast in our house. There was a story here and I wanted to find out what it was.

In the meantime, this little one needed to be taken care of. I was the oldest of four kids in our house. I was used to taking care of my younger siblings, since my parents worked as well. There were two mothers who stayed at home because they had just given birth and if we kids had any problems, we could always go to them. By now, this new little one trusted me. He was back at our table in the mornings.

One morning I found him sitting at the table with a note pinned to his little shirt. The note read, "My name is Danny. I am three years old. I speak Spanish. Thank you." Wow! He had a name. He was not talking because he did not understand our language. I was calling him Baby because I didn't know his name all this time. He would always go to his house after dinner. I thought his mom was home.

One evening I was curious and watched as he bravely went across the street and disappeared into the house. **Wait!** There were no lights in that house. Even if they were, he couldn't reach the switch. I told my mom that I was going over to check on Danny because there were no lights on in the house. I ran over to the house and went in, calling Danny's name, but got no answer. I looked through the house and could not find him.

I was praying and God said, "Look under his little bed."

I got down on the floor on my hands and knees and looked under the bed and I could see him curled in a little ball, shivering in the dark.

"Danny? Come here, baby," I said to him quietly.

He recognized my voice and reached for my hand. I pulled him out and squeezed him tight. He clung to me and did not cry, but he was really shaking. I rocked him, sang lullabies to him, and soon he was asleep. I put him in his mother's bed and went home to my house. I didn't think I could bring him home for the night, but I really wanted to keep him at our house so he would not be alone at age three.

I saw his mother coming out to wash her hair another day, so I went over to speak with her. She was so happy someone came to visit with her. I told her my name and she told me her name was Isabella. She did not speak much English but spoke enough for me to understand and piece together the mystery. They escaped here to the US from South America after her husband was killed. She had to leave her baby here in this community to go to a job someone had gotten for her, so she could take care of herself and her son. Someone had let her stay in the house but no utilities had been turned on. She didn't know how to shop in the stores or use the money to turn on the utilities in the house. She had no family here, no support no one to help her get around in this strange country. She did not understand the culture or the language and wanted to return home very badly. This was no way for her to live. She was frightened to be here in this strange country where she knew no one. She was frightened to leave her baby and he was frightened to be left alone, but he was a brave little soldier. I often wonder what she said to him.

They didn't have food. She brought home a little something from the job when she could hide it away in her purse to give little Danny. She could eat at the job. She thanked me for taking good care of her baby and asked God to bless me for doing that.

"I love little Danny," I said to her. "He's such a sweet baby."

She smiled through tears and said that he was her brave little soldier. We had a lovely conversation while she dried and brushed her hair that shined in the afternoon sun. She was twenty-three. She told me that the sun was very good for hair, and even back in South America she washed and brushed her hair out in the sun. It helped her hair to grow long and strong.

After that conversation, I told my parents when they came home, and we began sharing our food and whatever else we could give to help make them comfortable. I asked her if she could communicate with her family and friends in South America, to see if she could return safely. She said she would try.

A few weeks after that, I was out playing and saw another taxi drive up. She and Danny were standing in the front yard, waiting for me to notice. I did and went running over to them. She was smiling. She had gotten a letter and she was going to meet her family, who had managed to get to the Dominican Republic. They were going to be together again. Someone had sent the airfare for her. Danny was clinging to my leg, so I bent and picked him up as I had done so many times before. This time he hugged me and kissed me over and over on my cheeks to say goodbye. His mother came and hugged me too. She thanked me for my friendship, even though I was a little girl. She said that I was the best friend she had in this country. Tears came to her eyes as she thanked me for taking care of her brave little soldier.

Little Danny and I had become great friends even though he didn't speak English and I didn't speak Spanish. He was learning a few words here and there and I was learning a few words in Spanish. Mostly he was quiet, unless he was playing with me. Danny was the bravest little man I have ever seen. He did not scream, cry, throw tantrums or complain. He never stamped his little feet in frustration and anger, saying, "No!" He obeyed his mother even when he was scared or hungry, and even when she was not there to take him to go potty.

I will never forget that precious little face. I imagined that was what Christ was like when He was a little one. But Christ had His mother with Him all day and night. Little Danny didn't have his mother all day, she had to work. It must have broken her heart to have to leave him like she did, not knowing what would happen to him during the course of the day while she was gone. She was the one who had dressed him and brought him over to our house in the wee hours of the morning and sat him at our table to wait patiently and quietly for breakfast that first morning when I happened to see him sitting there. She had hoped he would be safe with us even though she had not met us. As God would have it, little Danny *was* safe with us. I just wished we could have done more to help. If I were older than seven years, I would have done more. I know it.

After more hugs and kisses and tears, Isabella and Danny got into the taxi and drove away to start their new life in the Dominican Republic, reunited with family. Yes, I pray that I will see them when Jesus comes again, where we will all live together in peace with Him, never to part again. where we will never need anything again because all we need will be given to us by God Himself. Where we will all speak the same language and understand each other perfectly.

When God leads, it might be to help a scared little toddler you don't know, when you are seven years old.

Chapter 18

WHEN GOD LEADS IT IS ALWAYS INTO A CLOSER RELATIONSHIP WITH HIM

As you can see from the events above, every time God led me in a certain direction, it was to help somebody...even if it was my own self. I always ended up growing closer to God in the process. The bottom line is that God loves us and wants us to have a relationship with Him that is closer than we can imagine. We don't really get it because our relationships here on planet Earth are sinful, disconnected, discombobulated, and flawed to distraction. So, we don't get it when God says He loves us. Huh? We don't know what that means.

When human beings say, "I love you," it could mean a plethora of things very different from what you may think it means. How confusing. What/who are we to believe? Even the Bible says in Jeremiah 17:9 that the heart is deceitful above all and desperately wicked. Who can know it? Man, if the Bible says *that,* who are *we* to try doing *anything* without God to guide us through this maze of life with its wicked tricks and turns? This is why I am taking the time to learn to stop and get counsel from the Most High, one true Creator God, who sees and knows everything. I listen for His directives before I make a move of any kind. This takes real practice, but don't give up. I'm not. You will be delighted at each outcome as I continue to be.

Look. Our great God left the splendors of heaven and came down to Earth, enemy territory, to endure constant harassment, ridicule, shame, spitting, torture and the most horrible death anyone could imagine. He did that for you and He did that for me, to get us back from the clutches of our old kidnapper. We are saved under one condition: we have to believe God **is** and accept His gift of what He **did** to save us. Then our conversations with Him will be easy, normal, and a delight.

Our relationship with God is personal and intensely intimate, more than any relationship we can have on the planet. Why? Because God knows us better than the pair who gave birth to us, or better than we know ourselves. God's love for us is supernatural. We just have to trust and believe because we have nothing to compare with that kind of love here where we live on planet Earth.

It is interesting to me that our supernatural God wants a closer-than-close relationship with us humans. What does that even mean? Do you know what that means? No? It's very hard to fathom because of who we are and where we live and how we choose to believe and what voices we choose to listen to. That is specifically the reason why God left us the Bible. His manuscript tells us the answers to all our questions and shows us who He is and what He is all about. We need to take a second and third look at this manuscript. It has not been protected all this time (centuries) for us to ignore it. Let's ask God to help us in the reading and understanding of His manuscript, the Bible, to bring us closer to Him. He will do that. I know this from my own experiences, a few of which I'm sharing with you now, because when God leads it is always to a closer relationship with Him.

Chapter 19

WHEN GOD LEADS IT MIGHT BE INTO BEING ALONE WITH HIM AT THE ZOO AGAIN!

I was in the Bronx, New York, after a particularly grueling day at work, when I heard God telling me to go to the zoo. Now it was a blistering hot summer in the city. Heat waves were visibly rising from the concrete and asphalt. All I wanted to do was go home to my apartment, take a shower, wash the city dirt out of my hair and skin, put on light, comfortable clothes, enjoy a cool refreshing drink, and relax. But I distinctly heard God telling me to head directly to the zoo.

"I want to show you something incredible," He said.

So, off to the zoo I went. Following the directions once I entered the gates, I couldn't believe my eyes and ears. God had led me to a space inside the zoo that was beautiful! Trees, brush and down a little embankment was the cutest little flowing stream that babbled along over some rocks and tree roots. It was hidden, private, cool, and refreshing. I visited the zoo often, as I really loved animals, but I had never ever noticed this place before.

"I want to spend some time with you here," God said.

"You are right again, Lord," I said. "This place is amazing!"

The city noises and the zoo noises were muted in this place. I only heard the voice of the singing brook and a few birds chirping in the trees above. It was cool and calming and I was wonderfully alone. God met me there. Our conversations were amazing. I couldn't wait for God to invite me to our secret place where we could be together in our private jungle setting in the middle of the city.

Often, Jesus would get away from the crowds of people to be alone with His Father in some solitary place. Away from all the distractions and noise, so they could share. Jesus always came away refreshed, with renewed strength of body, mind, and spirit.

That's what taking time alone with God will do for us, too. Then we can hear His voice more clearly and focus on what He is teaching us.

Whatever the picture of being alone is for you, take this time to get closer to God. If you are recently without a spouse, or if your children have left the nest and are out making their own way in the world, whatever your picture of being alone looks like, don't pull away from God. Move in closer to Him. He will do for you what He did for Jesus. He will renew your strength and give you wisdom and knowledge and power and courage to do what He asks of you at this special time of your life.

When God leads, sometimes it is into being alone, but He promises that He will *never* leave us! So, although we may be away from people for a time, God is **always** with us. God. Our protector, our provider, our guide, our sustainer, our teacher, our comfort, our healer, our way maker...shall I go on? Because you **know** I can. Our one God is **all that** and more. We have no need for a million other deities, our **one God** is more than enough power to take care of our every need. How awesome is that?

Anyway, I think you've got it. So, lean in hard and expect Him to come through for you, and I'm here to tell you that He will not disappoint.

When God leads, it might be to an amazingly beautiful place to be alone with Him.

Chapter 20

WHEN GOD LEADS IT MIGHT BE TO THROW A "B.Y.O.C. PARTY!"

Green, yellow, orange, and baby blue signs were in all the elevators in my building. Colorful Post-it Notes were on the entry doors of the selected apartments on the floor of my new living space. Why? Because God told me to do this. Yep. I woke up one morning, and during my early talks with God, He told me to get up and go to the store downstairs and purchase some Post-it Notes, some color printer paper and a roll of clear tape.

"We're going to throw a party," God said.

"Okaaay," I chuckled.

I bounced out of bed, got dressed and went to the store to purchase said items. Friend, if you don't know me and you don't know my friend Jesus, the one thing you need to know about *us* is that we love love, **love** a good party! While I'm getting to know Him more each day, I have learned that one of the first things He is going to do when we all get to heaven is to throw **the biggest welcome home party the universe has ever seen!** But please, don't get it twisted. This is not going to be a praise party like we have at some places now. Oh nooooo! **This** will be **God's "Welcome Home, Children," party!**

Nobody has ever seen a party like this one, and if you don't like parties now, I'm sorry for you. You may not make it to this one. Because there will be no party-poopers or wallflowers at **this party!** Everyone will be having the best time in the party spirit because we will be home with our Father forever, never to be separated ever, **ever** again. Oh, and don't worry about the not liking parties thing, because we will all be changed in a moment and in the twinkling of an eye at His coming, which means **now that you are changed, you will love to party like the rest of us!** Ha ha ha ha ha. Yes! Yes! **Yes!**

Okay. So I bought all the items, and once back in my apartment I asked God, "Now what?"

"Write this," God said. "You are invited to a B.Y.O.C. Party in Apartment #4B at 7:30 PM June 12, 1973. Please RSVP at (718) 555-5555. Looking forward to seeing you soon!"

"A **what** party?" I asked.

"A B.Y.O.C. party!" God said.

"Okay, Lord. I give up. What is a B.Y.O.C. party?" I asked.

"It is simply an acronym for Bring Your Own Chair. As you can see, we have no furniture in this room...or any other room in our apartment yet," God said.

I know He was chuckling, but I didn't hear that.

Oh, that's cute, I thought as I began to write the notes to go on the doors and in the elevators. As soon as I had finished the last note and poster, I darted out to place them. Later that evening, my phone began ringing, with curious neighbors wondering if this was some kind of joke. I told them that it was real and what the acronym stood for. We had a good laugh and they all said they would be there.

I was in the elevator one evening before the party date when someone read the poster out loud.

"Don't forget to RSVP for the BYOC!" they read.

Then they asked out loud: "What is a BYOC?" One of the persons in the elevator ripped down the poster and said, half under his breath, "It's not for you if you have to ask!" I was smiling at this reaction and figured he was one of my neighbors. Remember, I didn't know any of these people, though I lived in the same building as they did, but all *that* was about to change. Yessiree, it was about to change.

The evening of the event, my phone kept ringing to confirm that the party was still on. Some asked if they could come early. Of course, I said yes. Soon my doorbell began ringing, announcing the arrival of the partygoers. When I opened the door, people began streaming in carrying all kinds of chairs and large pillows to sit on. After the last person came in, my front room was filled with neighbors I was about to meet with my ice-breaker games, which left everyone howling with laughter. The food was delicious, the drinks were amazing, all-virgin-no-alcohol.

The music was "off the chain!" as we used to say back in the day. All Gospel music. One of the guys who came in asked if that was Gospel music playing.

I said, "Yes, because I'm a church lady!"

I appointed him as our DJ for the party. He worked it! We had a wonderful, fun time getting to know each other. All my neighbors wanted to know when the **next** party would be. We decided we would do this twice a month, and after a couple of months they decided to put themselves on the calendar for hosting the party. We became a family that night.

The next day after the first party, I came home to a door full of posted notes, all telling me about the fun we had meeting each other, which put a big smile on my face. They all felt so good the next day that we all decided all our parties would be plant-based foods and virgin drinks. Easy-peasy and fun.

My neighbors began learning a new lifestyle from watching and interacting with me, and it was so much **funnnn** teaching them in that way. The poem, *Sermons We See,* by Edgar Guest, was in motion in real time right on my floor in my apartment building. If you are not familiar with this poem, it's public domain, so I'm going to put it right here for you. Enjoy!

I'd rather see a sermon than to hear one any day:
I'd rather one should walk with me than merely tell the way.
The eye's a better pupil and more willing than the ear,
Fine counsel is confusing, but example's always clear;
And the best of all the preachers are the ones who live their creeds,
For to see good put in action is what everybody needs.

I soon can learn to do if you'll let me see it done;
I can watch your hands in action but your tongue too fast may run.
And the lecture you deliver may be very wise and true,
But I'd rather get my lessons by observing what you do;
For I might misunderstand you and the high advice you give,
But there's no misunderstanding how you act and how you live.

When I see a deed of kindness, I am eager to be kind.

84

When a weaker brother stumbles and a strong man stays behind
Just to see if he can help him, then the wish grows strong in me
To become as big and thoughtful as I know that friend to be.
And all travelers can witness that the best of guides today
Is not the one who tells them, but the one who shows the way.

One good man teaches many, men believe what they behold;
One deed of kindness noticed is worth forty that are told.
Who stands with men of honor learns to hold his honor dear,
For right living speaks a language which to every one is clear.
Though an able speaker charms me with his eloquence, I say,
I'd rather see a sermon than to hear one, any day.

This poem is public domain now, but I read it when I was six years old. It made a great impression on my young mind and how I choose to live today. I try to live like Jesus wants me to live, and if others see and want to learn how to live that way, well, praise Him!

We had many more BYOC parties that were so much fun, when it was time for me to move to another location, I made them promise to keep the party flavor going. They promised they would.

Did I tell you that Jesus loves a good party? Well, another party idea that He gave me was the Church Pew Party. When I arrived at church and took my seat, I would hand out invitations to those who sat on the same pew as me in church. It was an invitation to dinner at my place after church, and all who wanted to come should meet me after the service on the organ side of the sanctuary to get directions and/or follow me home. Of course, God helped me fix food and dessert in advance for as many who would come. We had a great time getting to know each other better. I passed the plan on to other members, and they started having pew parties too. Most of our guests stayed till night and we would have worship to close the Sabbath, then play games or just talk or sing until they left, one by one. Good times.

What is God leading you to do for Him? Are you listening? Can you hear? Are you willing to do exactly what He is telling you to do? Practice living in His presence. I am sure you will hear Him speak to you.

Blessings, my friend. Listen closely.

When God Leads...what might the chapter title be for you? You're writing your own book right now. Chapter by chapter, page by page, line by line. Stop and think back on the things that have happened in your own life that could only have been God who saved, directed, healed, etc. Think. I know you will come up with many times when God intervened, even if you didn't know it was Him taking care of you. My personal experience is that God **does** speak. And God **does** lead. God loves me and I know He loves you too!

"Shhhh! Can you hear that?"

Listen closely, it might be God speaking and wanting to lead you somewhere special and wonderful! Hear **Him** today and **follow** where He leads.

CPSIA information can be obtained
at www.ICGtesting.com
Printed in the USA
LVHW080312290422
717389LV00012B/257